Anowa

Ama Ata Aidoo

Pupils' edition for BECE e[illegible]artin Okyere Owusu and Benjamin Okyere Asante

PEARSON
Longman

Pearson Education Limited
Edinburgh Gate
Harlow
Essex CM20 2JE
England
and Associated Companies throughout the World

www.longman.com

ISBN 0 582 81895 8

Printed in China
EPC/01

Prepared for publication by the Pen and Ink Book Company Ltd
Typeset in Palatino and Ocean Sans MT

Contents

About the author

Ama Ata Aidoo is a writer of poems, plays, short stories and novels. She is also a consultant on education and gender issues. She was born at Saltpond on the Gold Coast, now Ghana, in 1942.

She graduated with a B.A. from the University of Ghana and worked in the United States of America where she held a fellowship in creative writing at Stanford University. She also served as Research Fellow at the Institute of African Studies, University of Ghana at Legon, and as a lecturer at the University of Cape Coast. She has also been Secretary of Education in Ghana.

Aidoo's works include: *The Dilemma of a Ghost* (1965); *Anowa*, her second play, published in 1969; *Our Sister Killjoy* (1977); *No Sweetness Here* (1970); *Someone Talking to Someone* (1985); and *An Angry Letter in January* (1992).

Her novel *Changes* (1991) won the 1992 Commonwealth Writers Prize for Best Book (Africa) and Aidoo held the position of Lecturer in English at the University of Cape Coast, where, through hard work, commitment and dedication to her academic and research duties, she rose to her present position of Professor.

Her first play, *Dilemma of a Ghost*, achieved instant international acclaim, especially for her creative use of language and down-to-earth, believable African situations. That play and *Anowa* have both featured, on several occasions, as set books for the West African Examinations Council.

In her plays, Aidoo portrays women with very strong personalities who, contrary to social and cultural expectations or norms, insist on expressing their views on matters that affect them, especially marriage.

Sometimes one can hear Aidoo's voice in her female characters, speaking out against social injustice towards women. In *Anowa*, the following line, spoken by the oppressed Anowa, branded a witch for speaking her mind, suggests the writer's strong protest against society:

> Someone should have taught me how to grow up to be a woman. (p.77)

In most of her creative works, Aidoo is concerned with the questions of marriage, womanhood, children, the family, and the way these are affected by wider society, attitudes and cultural practices.

The Play

Setting

Any play, story or novel is placed in a particular time-frame and geographical location. This is done so that the audience or reader can understand why characters behave in certain ways. It also helps the audience or reader not to misjudge the actions of the characters. For instance, the audience should be able to determine the century, period of time or year when the action of the drama takes place. Is it in the 20th Century, or 1961, or the period of the Great War? Is it the present time? Some plays are even placed in the future. The place, which is as important as the time, could be any part of the world. For instance, it could be West Africa, which is so big, or Ghana, which is smaller, or Tamale, which is even smaller still. It is important to know where the drama takes place, so that the audience can know the religious, traditional, political or social practices of the people. The time and place in which the action of the drama, story or novel occurs is known as the **setting**.

The play, *Anowa*, is set in the mid-19th Century, the period between 1800 and 1870, when human beings were sold and bought as slaves (p.51). This was also the time when the political head of the land was the Governor. The larger area where the drama occurs is West Africa, which was then referred to as the Guinea Coast (p.69). The actual location of the play is in the Akan area of the Gold Coast, which is now Ghana. This is shown by the names of people, places and objects in the play.

The names of Anowa, Kofi Ako, Abena Badua, Kobina Osam (p.35), Abakrampahene Kokroko (p.84), Takoa (p.73), Panyin-Na-Kakra (p.76) and others are names peculiar to the Akan of the Gold Coast (Ghana). Also, places such as Atandasu (p.45), Oguaa, Tantri (p.78), Yebi (p.61), Abura (p.62), the names of objects like kente (p.69) and beads (p.47), and the mention of the Nsona clan, show that the place is in the Akan area, and, more exactly, in Fanti land.

The play actually starts in Yebi, a village in the state of Abura. This is a coastal area where the continually roaring sea provides the people with an abundance of fish. Along the coast are forts and castles built by the 'pale men' (white men) for the cruel trade in human beings (the Slave Trade).

After the Prologue, in which the scene is set, Phase One begins in the cottage of Maami Badua and Papa Osam. It is evening, when families prepare their evening meals.

The action of Phase Two begins on a highway that passes through a rain forest and ends at Oguaa (Cape Coast).

In Phase Three, we are taken to the hall of the big house built in Oguaa by Kofi Ako.

Beliefs and Practices

The people in the play believe in their gods and worship their ancestral spirits. The living respect the spirits of the dead as well as their traditional gods. For instance, Osam prays to them when he says:

> And may the ancestral spirits help me, but what man would I order from the heavens to please the difficult eye of my daughter Anowa? (p.31)

In a conversation with his wife, Badua, Osam gives us a hint about Anowa's birth:

> Osam: What is wrong with priestesses?
> Badua: I don't say there is anything wrong with them.
> Osam: Did you not consult them over and over again when you could not get a single child from your womb to live beyond one day? (p.31)

At the end of the Prologue, the Old Woman declares:

> And the gods will surely punish Abena Badua for refusing to let a born priestess dance! (p.26)

In other words, if the people disobey their own gods and spirits, they are most likely to face disastrous consequences.

Culturally, this society is dominated by men, and even ideas from women are considered strange. For instance, the Old Woman declares, at the end of Phase Two:

> As the sourest yam
> Is better than the sweetest guava,
> The dumbest man is

Always better than a woman.
Or *he* thinks he is!
And so Kofi shall teach Anowa
He is a man! (p.64)

In Yebi society, the elderly have control over the younger generation. The Old Woman hints at this when she asks, about Anowa:

When was this infant born,
That would teach us all what to do?
Who is she to bring us new rules to live by?
It is good she said she was not coming back to Yebi,
But if she so much as crosses the stream
That lies at the mouth of the road,
We shall show her that
Little babies only cry for food
When hungry,
But do not instruct their elders how to tend a farm …
(p.64)

It is a taboo for a young person to disrespect an elder. It amounts to a disturbance of the natural order of things. In the play, Anowa is accused of going her own way and disregarding advice from her parents about her marriage. The Old Man says, in the Prologue:

A child of several incarnations,
She listens to her own tales
Laughs at her own jokes and
Follows her own advice. (p.25)

Characters (people) in the play

People in a play are called **characters**. Each of them has been created from the playwright's thoughts and observation of all kinds of people. These characters are given life through the way they are introduced. Are they men or women, boys or girls, young or old? What is their individual way of behaviour? How do they speak or walk? Are they patient, hot-tempered, proud, haughty, humble, lazy, hard-working and so on?

Each character has been given a duty to perform in order to move the action forward as well as to develop the **theme** or message.

Some characters have major roles, others minor. **Major** means that they have a lot to do and say. They carry most of the dialogue and actions, and are present in most of the scenes. Major characters are sometimes called 'principal' characters.

Minor characters play small, but often important, roles. They may not have much to say or do; or they may appear briefly in one or two scenes. But they are also important, because without them the action cannot move forward. Sometimes they have important information to give to the major characters. It is important to remember that a character may be bad or good as a person, but play a major or minor role.

In trying to understand the total importance of characters in a play, therefore, it is necessary to look at two aspects of each character: their nature (or human qualities), and their role, or how they contribute to the success of the whole play.

Also, in judging any character as good or bad, we must be able to give reasons for our opinion. We can only do this when we find out what the character says about himself or herself, what he or she says about others and, most importantly, what the character actually does in the play.

Anowa

Anowa is the main character in this tragic drama. The main character in a play is called the **protagonist**. Because Anowa is a woman, she can also be called the **heroine**. From what the Old Man and the Old Woman, neighbours, parents (Osam and Badua) say about her, and from her quick attack on her parents when they disagree with her choice of husband, Anowa shows clearly that she is hot-tempered (easily aroused to anger). We can see that she is:

- proud and arrogant
- hot-tempered and impulsive (she makes hasty decisions)
- disrespectful and saucy
- wilful (she does what she likes)
- adventurous
- hard-working.

The first impression the author gives us about Anowa is that she is proud, arrogant and a spoilt child. Right from the beginning of the play we are told by the Old Woman and the Old Man that she has refused to marry any of the sturdy men who asked for her hand in marriage and that she laughs at her own jokes, listens to her own tales and follows her own advice. In other words, she does not value anyone else's opinion.

Anowa's pride leads her to choose her own husband even against the wish of her parents, and her mother fails in all her attempts to make her change her mind. Anowa's not accepting any of the men recommended by her parents and choosing her own husband against her parents' wishes is, in the traditional African setting, seen as a taboo.

Anowa's role as a child and also a wife helps in the development of the play, as her role contributes to the whole tragedy. As a child, she is expected to be obedient, not only to her parents, but also to other elderly people. In fact, we see that the way she behaves makes people fear her and keep their distance from her.

In the African setting we know that girls are given in marriage by their parents and family, and that it is believed that this brings blessings to the couple; but with Anowa, we see how she chooses her own husband, thus gaining a curse, rather than the blessings of her parents. Later, she resists the very man she chose above all the others, when she feels he is not doing what is right. Anowa can therefore be said to be an extremist and it is that part of her character that the playwright uses to develop the play.

Kofi Ako

Kofi Ako is Anowa's counterpart. He is at first a protagonist, but later turns against her. He is portrayed as handsome, and the impression Abena Badua gives about him is that he is lazy. In his character, we see him as not only lazy, but also masterful. He does not respect the views of women. He does not behave well, as he does not ask Anowa's hand in marriage from her parents.

Kofi Ako is selfish, as he uses his manhood to acquire slaves and wealth without thinking of his wife's well-being or happiness. Anowa strongly opposes his consulting with oracles, but we realise in the end that he does not listen to his wife's advice. He is therefore responsible for their childlessness. Kofi Ako fails in his role as a husband to make his wife happy.

Kofi Ako is also seen as arrogant. He does not listen to any advice, especially when it comes from women. He demands of Anowa, 'Who are you to tell me what I must do or not do?' Also, when Anowa opposes his suggestion of buying slaves he tells her, 'Besides, you are only talking like a woman.' He is the type of person who wants things done his way, no matter the cost, and so he ignores Anowa's advice and acquires great wealth, buying slaves and stopping working himself. Kofi Ako is a man who likes to have an easy life without sweat or toil.

Kofi Ako's laziness and arrogance make him reject his wife's advice. This brings him shame, as it becomes clear that he has exchanged his masculinity (manhood) for wealth and slaves. Anowa's exposure of his impotence leads him to shoot himself.

Badua

Badua's actions show that she is a concerned mother, but complains a lot. When various people suggest that she should apprentice Anowa to the priestesses she objects:

> They counsel with spirits;
> They read into other men's souls;
> They swallow dogs' eyes …
> I want my child
> To be a human woman
> Marry a man,
> Tend a farm
> And be happy to see her
> Peppers and her onions grow.
> A woman like her
> Should bear children
> Many children,
> So she can afford to have
> One or two die. (p.32)

She is very insistent and a firm decision-maker. She says:

> I have said it and I will say it again and again and again! I am not going to turn my only daughter into a dancer priestess. (p.31)

She is very clear that she does not want Kofi Ako as a son-in-law. She is very selective and she also upholds tradition.

At first, Badua, as a concerned mother, bitterly laments Anowa's refusal to get married, even six years after puberty. She also wonders:

> If I do not worry about this, what shall I worry about? (p.30)

As Anowa, having chosen Kofi Ako, leaves Yebi, swearing never to return, Badua bows her head and weeps quietly. (p.39)

Badua says that she herself is 'just an unlucky woman' (p.37), but that for Anowa 'A captainship in the army should not be beyond her when the time is ripe!' (p.32)

The Old Woman says that:

> Others think that her mother, Badua, has spoilt her shamefully … Badua should tell her daughter that the sapling breaks with bending that will not grow straight. (pp.25–26)

We can see from this that others are suggesting that Badua is responsible for Anowa's negative tendencies.

Boy and Girl (slaves)

These two are young slaves adopted as 'Son' and 'Daughter' by Kofi Ako and Anowa. They clean and sweep the rooms of the house and work on the farm with other slave children.

Although the Boy appears briefly on stage in Phase Two (pp.56–57), it is in Phase Three, when he and the Girl come to clean a room, that something important happens. The Girl looks like the young Anowa. In the author's description:

> She resembles Anowa of a long time ago. She is dressed in a one-piece cloth wrapped around her. She, too, looks like a wild one … suddenly she stops and just stands dreamily. (p.72)

The Girl accidentally breaks one of the 'decorative plates'. This action may be a **symbol** (standing for something) or an omen (a warning). It could mean the break-up of the marriage between Anowa and Kofi Ako.

An important part of the roles of the Boy and (especially) the Girl, is that they tell us a lot about the situation in the house of Ako and Anowa. For example, the Girl says that Anowa moves about the house 'like a ghost' and that she talks to herself (p.73). This shows us that Anowa is not happy and does not have peace of mind.

The Girl also says that people in the town are accusing Anowa of being a witch, because she looked hard at a baby and the child became ill with convulsions. The baby's mother, Takoa, has been spreading the news where the women smoke their fish. The Girl also believes that Anowa is unhappy because she has no child of her own.

When the Boy suggests (p.76) that maybe 'Father' (Kofi Ako) may take the Girl for a wife, her reply is very interesting. She says: '*Chiaa*, *aa*, that man who is afraid of women?' She is going to reveal more facts when the Boy chases her away.

Their conversation reveals that there is much unhappiness in the couple's home; that Anowa is not happy and that Kofi Ako is afraid of women.

Osam

Osam is the husband of Badua and father of Anowa, but he appears to be more interested in producing children than in taking a serious interest in their upbringing. He says to his wife:

> You know that I am a man and getting daughters married is not one of my duties. Getting them born, aha! But not finding them husbands. (p.31)

He represents those men who believe that the uncles and aunts of their children should bear the responsibility of caring for them. He shows a lot of impatience when Badua expresses concern about Anowa's unwillingness to get married. He calls her worries 'complaints'. In other words, Osam simply does not care.

Right from the beginning of the play, Osam disagrees with his wife on anything to do with Anowa. He is quite the opposite of Badua in terms of family care. He believes in the 'matrilineal' system of family care, whereby fathers take greater care of their nieces and nephews (i.e. their sisters' children) than of their own. Osam can therefore be described as a 'passive' parent, while his wife is the 'active' one. In drama, Osam's contrasting nature and role make him a **foil** or **contrast** to Badua.

The-Mouth-That-Eats-Salt-And-Pepper

These two characters – an Old Man and an Old Woman – are described by the author at the beginning of the Prologue. The Old Woman is described as 'wizened' (dried up), while the Old Man is described as:

> *... serene and everything about him is more orderly. He enters quietly and leaves after his last statements have been made.* (p.23)

They represent the opposite sides of ideas: male – female; serene (peaceful)

– wild; healthy – sickly; solid (firm) – wandering (unstable). They have different opinions about things, but between them they provide important information and pass comments, fair or unfair, on Anowa's character and the influences that have made her as she is.

The two are a kind of 'Chorus'. They introduce the play by giving us the geographical, political and historical background (see the *Setting* section on page 5).

They express possible reasons for the state of affairs, putting the blame on characters, based on gossip or hearsay. For example, the Old Man describes Anowa as 'unfortunate' and 'not a girl to meet every day'. In other words, she is strange and unusual. There is something wrong with her. The Old Woman adds her opinion to that of the Old Man. They talk a lot about Anowa. Badua's remarks on Anowa's fate suggest that the two old people represent the entire community who gossip endlessly about her.

They give us the exact point in time when the action of the play begins:

> It is now a little less than thirty years
> When the lords of our Houses
> Signed that piece of paper –
> The Bond of 1844 they call it –
> Binding us to the white men
> Who came from beyond the horizon. (p.26)

At the end of each Phase they share with the audience their views about what has gone on between Anowa and Kofi Ako. It is the Old Woman who tells us that Kofi Ako has shot himself and Anowa has drowned herself. Then she tries to give reasons, and to hand out blame, for the downfall of the two characters. But the Old Man cautions us not to be too hasty. He says:

> There is surely one thing we know how to do very well. And that is assigning blame when things go wrong. (p.89)

It is the Old Man who speaks the last words in the play.

Panyin-Na-Kakra

These are twin brothers who fan Kofi Ako's empty chair. Anowa tells them to stop doing so and to go and play with the other children. It shows Anowa to be a woman who has good feelings towards children. In fact it shows her as a 'mother' even though she does not have a child of her own.

The twins' actions show how Kofi Ako has become so heartless that he makes children fan his chair even when he is not sitting on it.

Themes

The messages we receive from a play such as *Anowa* are referred to as **themes**. When we read or watch a play (or read any short story, novel, or poem) we must ask ourselves: 'What message is the writer sending us? What kind of message is it? Where can we find it? How do we express or state it? Is it a moral message or one that gives us an important aspect of life to think about?' The message may even be about a social or cultural practice which the writer disapproves of. It can also show how certain people can believe in something so strongly that they are even prepared to suffer for it when they are forced to give up their stand.

The reader or audience (people watching the play in performance) can get the whole message (or theme) only after finishing enjoying the entire play or drama. For instance, if we stop reading *Anowa* halfway through or leave the theatre before the performance comes to an end, we shall not be in a position to get an accurate and complete message. We shall read or see how *Anowa* begins, but we will not know what happens to Anowa and her husband in the end. In other words, we will not have a complete picture or story from which we can understand the messages provided by the writer.

Themes in Anowa

We can see several **themes** in *Anowa*. These include:

1 The result or consequences of disobeying one's parents out of pride.
2 Happiness in a family cannot be bought with riches and wealth – love and care are more important.
3 Human beings, especially children and those we call slaves, must all be treated with dignity.

We will consider each of the above themes (lessons) carefully and show why they are true.

1 *The result or consequences of disobeying one's parents out of pride.*

Anowa is said to be a very beautiful girl, but she is full of pride. This makes her refuse to marry any of the strongly-built young men in the village who ask for her hand in marriage.

Instead, she rejects them all and chooses Kofi Ako, a young man who is considered lazy and good for nothing. When her mother, Badua, refuses to accept Kofi Ako as a son-in-law, Anowa becomes angry, quarrels with her mother and even calls her a 'witch'. She says:

> Please, Mother, remove your witch's mouth from our marriage. (p.38)

For calling her mother a witch, Anowa brings a curse upon herself. After getting rid of her feelings with insults and unpleasant, quarrelsome talk, she decides to leave their town, Yebi, with her husband but without the blessing of her parents.

As she departs, her mother's last farewell is not a blessing, but a curse. She says:

> Let her go. And may she walk well. (p.39)

Anowa's answer to her mother is equally bad:

> Mother, I shall walk so well that I will not find my feet back here again. (p.39)

These words portray a girl who does not show respect to her parents. The Old Man and the Old Woman, who introduce the action of the play, describe her as a spoilt child, a witch, one who carries herself 'stiffly' and who does not listen to anyone but herself.

This pride soon reduces her to a very unhappy person in her marriage to Kofi Ako, once the two have settled in Oguaa and Kofi has begun to get rich. They often quarrel over the way they should do things. Anowa likes to work. In fact, she says:

> I like this work. I like being on the roads. (p.50)

She hates being idle while slaves do all the work. Kofi Ako, however, prefers his wife to live like a queen, while he increases his wealth.

When Anowa finds out that her husband had secretly consulted diviners about his loss of manhood she does not hesitate to let the whole world know. She yells at him in public:

> Kofi, are you dead? [*Pause*] Kofi is your manhood gone? I mean, you are like a woman. [*Pause*] Kofi, there is not hope any more, is there? [*Pause*] Kofi … tell me, is that why I must leave you? That you have exhausted your masculinity acquiring slaves and wealth?

> [*Silence*]
> Why didn't you want me to know? You could have told me. Because we were friends. Like brother and sister. You just did not want me to know? And the priest said it was my fault. That I ate your manhood up? Why did he say I did it? Out of envy? Did he not tell you that perhaps you had consumed it up yourself acquiring wealth and slaves?
> [KOFI *looks around and sees the peeping eyes. He is horrified. He gestures to* ANOWA *who doesn't know what is happening and goes on talking. He makes an attempt to go away and then sits down again. The slaves disappear.*]
> Now I know. So that is it. My husband is a woman now. [*She giggles.*] He is a corpse. He is dead wood. But less than dead wood because at least, that sometimes grows mushrooms … Why didn't you want me to know? (pp.86–87)

The shame of this disgrace sends Kofi Ako to commit suicide by shooting himself. After that, Anowa drowns herself in the river.

This 'tragic' or sad end happens as a result of Anowa's refusing to listen to her parents' advice and allowing pride to dictate her choice.

2 *Happiness in a family cannot be bought with riches and wealth – love and care are more important.*

Once Anowa and Kofi Ako have left Yebi to go to Oguaa, the only time they seem happy is when, on the road (path), they show love, care and affection as Kofi Ako protects Anowa with plantain leaves and animal skins. Kofi shows a lot of care for Anowa, and the two laugh happily at each other's jokes. Kofi displays his physical strength, and talks of Anowa's beauty.

But this show of love and care is short-lived; for when Kofi Ako becomes very wealthy he lives like a king, carried back and forth in a sedan chair, dressed in rich royal cloth. Even his empty throne is fanned by young twin boys, so that the air around it will be cool enough for their master's comfort.

In spite of this outward show of riches and power, Kofi is not a happy man. He does not care for Anowa any more; he neglects her completely as a wife, leaving her to wander about as a depressed, lonely, almost mad woman with nothing worthwhile to do. When Anowa complains about Kofi's lifestyle, he calls her a witch and threatens to send her back to Yebi. Anowa has sworn never to go back there.

Finally when, out of disappointment or frustration, Anowa exposes Kofi's impotence, he shoots himself. This shows that wealth, money, riches, property and so on cannot buy happiness in a family.

3 *Human beings, especially children and those we call slaves, must all be treated with dignity.*

Some of the actions in this play suggest that the playwright disapproves of the way children are ill-treated by some adults who, because they are rich, buy them from their poor parents. Such children are made to perform tasks that are very bad. For example, there are the two boys whose duty it is to fan Kofi Ako's chair even when he is not sitting on it. Anowa does not like the idea at all and tells them to stop and go away. She says:

> Poor children, I feel like picking them up and carrying them on my back. (p.76)

Meanwhile, Kofi Ako deals in slaves and has acquired many of them to work for him. Some of them even carry him in a sedan chair in and out of his house every day. Even our traditional Kings and Chiefs are carried in sedan chairs only on special occasions such as festivals and other important celebrations. In fact, Kofi Ako treats these children and slaves without dignity, a situation society must reject and condemn. Because of this behaviour, Kofi Ako suffers in the end, when his true self is exposed.

Style

(Dramatic Elements)

Conflict

This drama has been made interesting by the use of different types of **conflict**. A conflict is a clash between two opposing forces. Sometimes it is a fight or a quarrel; it may also be a struggle between characters. Conflict produces tension, and creates anxiety in the audience or reader.

We learn from the Old Woman in the Prologue that, because Anowa has refused to marry any man from Yebi who has asked for her hand, almost the whole society is against her. She is the subject of gossip.

This type of conflict is known as Man (Anowa) against Group (the Yebi people).

The next conflict is between Anowa and her parents, especially her mother, Badua. When Anowa comes home to announce to her parents that she intends to marry Kofi Ako, a serious quarrel develops. There are bitter exchanges between mother and daughter.

This type of conflict is known as Man (Anowa) against Man (Badua).

Another type of conflict in the play is where Man (Kofi Ako and Anowa) is in conflict with Nature. As the two of them are on the Highway, at the beginning of Phase Two, they encounter very stormy weather. There is so much lightning, thunder and rain, that Kofi Ako describes the night as 'fearful'. It is so cold that the two of them shiver terribly. The rain also makes some of their animal skins rot. Kofi Ako fears that if such weather continues, Anowa will become ill. The weather only improves on the following day.

There is also an inner conflict in the drama. It is known as a conflict of Man against Himself, and is the most dangerous type of all. This is because, before a person realises that he is in conflict with himself, it has almost destroyed him. Kofi Ako has gone for medicine (juju) and has exchanged his manhood for wealth and slaves. He has tried all along to keep this a secret. The fear that one day people may know about it worries him, and whenever Anowa suggests that he should marry another woman, he becomes disturbed and angry.

Towards the end of the play, when Kofi Ako realises that Anowa has given away the secret of his impotence, he goes quietly out and shoots himself dead.

Anowa also has an inner conflict. The thoughts that Kofi Ako has made slaves of fellow human beings, that she has no children, that she should have become a priestess, and that their marriage has broken apart, make her drown herself instead of going back to Yebi.

Contrast

Contrast comes from the differences between two objects. These differences can be to do with the appearance of characters or to do with their opinions. For instance, Kofi Ako is tall and broad, while Anowa is a small person. Throughout the drama the couple have different opinions. Kofi Ako thinks that they should buy slaves to help them in their trade, while Anowa has a strong dislike for the idea. She thinks it is evil to make slaves of fellow human beings. When Kofi Ako has become very rich, he dresses and behaves like a king, while Anowa still wears her old clothes and goes about barefooted. This difference is part of the reason why Kofi Ako wants to send Anowa away.

Climax

A **climax** happens when tension in the play rises to a very high point, for example, if there is nearly a fight between two opposing characters, or if a main character takes a dangerous decision. When Anowa announces to her parents that she has decided to marry Kofi Ako, tension immediately rises in the house. This develops into a quarrel to the point where mother and daughter almost hit each other.

Later, the marriage between Kofi Ako and Anowa becomes very sour. As they express their disappointment in each other the tension in the house rises, and when Anowa discovers and reveals Kofi Ako's impotence, the tension becomes unbearable and Kofi Ako shoots himself.

Irony

Irony is a situation where there is a difference between expectation and what actually happens. There are three types of irony. These are **verbal**, **situational**, and **dramatic** irony.

Verbal Irony
Verbal irony describes a statement whose intended meaning is opposite to the words spoken. When Badua says 'Let her go. And may she walk well.', does she really wish Anowa well?

Situational Irony
In this kind of irony, what characters expect and hope turns out to be the opposite of what actually happens. For instance, Anowa expects and hopes that her marriage with Kofi Ako is going to be perfect. She even tells her mother that she is going to help Kofi Ako to 'do something with his life' (p.38). But as the play continues, we learn how she has come to suffer at the hands of Kofi Ako. She is finally so disappointed that she drowns herself.

Dramatic Irony
In dramatic irony, the audience is aware that the truth is different from what the characters believe. For instance, in this drama, the Boy and the Girl believe that Anowa has no children of her own because she is barren and a witch, but the audience know that the real reason is that Kofi Ako has exchanged his manhood for wealth and slaves.

Symbolism

A **symbol** is something that has its own nature, but also stands for something else. A flag, for example, is a piece of coloured cloth, but it stands for a nation. Symbolism in drama, therefore, is the representation of ideas by physical objects.

The writer uses symbols in **Anowa** to make simple certain difficult ideas. There are many examples, including the stormy night, the breaking of the decorative plate, the fanning of an empty chair and the different types of clothing worn at various times by the characters.

Language

The play is written in English, but the writer has localised it by using **transliteration**. This is the use of a kind of English to match exactly certain local expressions. There are several examples in *Anowa*. When the Old Man describes Anowa's beauty, he uses the expression, 'Someone's-Thin-Thread' (p.25). This is a local expression, rendered directly into English.

Another example is when Anowa says: 'Please, Mother, remove your witch's mouth from our marriage' (p.38).

Also, in the conversation between Anowa and Kofi Ako in Phase Two, the whole of Anowa's response to Kofi Ako is a transliteration.

> Kofi Ako: Your mood is on. [*He stretches his left arm forward and looks at it intently.*]
>
> Anowa: [*Giggling*] What mood? You are always funny. My nothing is on. It is just that when I throw my eyes into the future, I do not see myself there. (p.58)

Other examples of transliteration in the play include:

> My mouth is at the dung heap. (p.45)
> I thank your mouth. (p.45)
>
> And is that a good thing to say about your own bowel-begotten child? (p.53)

Certain Ghanaian proverbs are also used in the play. In Phase One, when Osam and Badua are talking about Anowa not being sent to become a priestess, Osam tells Badua:

> And a prophet with locked mouth is neither a prophet nor a man.

> Besides, the yam that will burn, shall burn, boiled or roasted. (p.33)

At the end of Phase One, the Old Woman says:

> Badua should have told her daughter that the infant which tries its milk teeth on every bone and stone, grows up with nothing to eat dried meat with. (p.41)

Other proverbs used in the drama include:

> Some of us feel that the best way to sharpen a knife is not to whet one side of it only. (Old Man, p.40)
>
> They say that however good for licking the back of your hand is, it would never be like your palms. (Kofi Ako, p.49)
>
> Kofi, one stops wearing a hat only when the head has fallen off. (Anowa, p.57)
>
> The string of orphan beads might look better on the wrist of the leopard but it is the antelope who has lost his mother. (Anowa, p.76)

Local Expressions

Certain expressions in the Fanti language have also been used in the play. This language has been used to maintain the true strength, power and beauty of the words. If these words were to be expressed in English, the spirit of their meaning would be lost. A few of them are as follows:

> Nkabasroto and bubas – different kinds of Kaba dress. (p.75)
> Nanaam Mpow – Elders' sacred forest. (p.84)
> Dué, dué, dué – You have my sympathy. (p.88)
> Odomankoma – Our Creator. (p.23)
> Nana Bosompo – The Sea God. (p.24)

Anowa

For my mother
'Aunt Abasema'
who told a story and sang a song

Cast

OLD MAN } *Being The-Mouth-That-Eats*
OLD WOMAN } *Salt-And-Pepper*

A MAN AND A WOMAN: *who don't say a word*
ANOWA: *a young woman who grows up*
KOFI AKO: *her man who expands*
OSAM: *her father who smokes his pipe*
BADUA: *her mother who complains at the beginning and cries at the end*
BOY: *a young slave, about twenty years old*
GIRL: *a young slave girl*
PANYIN-NA-KAKRA: *a pair of boy twins whose duty it is to fan an empty chair*
HORNBLOWER
OTHER MEN AND WOMEN: *slaves, carriers, hailing women, drummers, messengers, townspeople*

Prologue

[*Enter* THE-MOUTH-THAT-EATS-SALT-AND-PEPPER.

OLD MAN *always enters first, from the left side of the auditorium.* OLD WOMAN *from the right. Each leaves in the same direction. She is wizened, leans on a stick and her voice is raspy with asthma and a life-time of putting her mouth into other people's affairs. She begins her speeches when she is half-way in and ends them half-way out. Her entries are announced by the thumping of her stick, and whenever she is the last of the two to leave the stage, her exit is marked by a prolonged coughing. She is never still and very often speaks with agitation, waving her stick and walking up and down the lower stage. He is serene and everything about him is more orderly. He enters quietly and leaves after his last statements have been made. The two should never appear or move onto the upper stage. There is a block of wood lying around on which the* OLD WOMAN *sometimes sits.*]

OLD MAN: Here in the state of Abura,
Which must surely be one of the best pieces of land
Odomankoma, our creator, has given to man,
Everything happens in moderation:
The sun comes out each day,
But its heat seldom burns our crops;
Rains are good when they fall
And Asaase Efua the earth-goddess gives of herself
To them that know the seasons;
Streams abound, which like all gods
Must have their angry moments and swell,
But floods are hardly known to living memory.
Behind us to the north, Aburabura
Our beautiful lonely mountain sits with her neck to the
skies,
Reminding us that all of the earth is not flat.

The action of the play is around the 1870s, almost thirty years after the Bond of 1844 which brought about European domination. We hear that the people of this land were not good fighters, especially in wars with their kinsmen from the North. That was why their leaders sought the help and protection of the Europeans on the coast. The result of this was, sadly, that they lost their independence, and many were led to depend on the 'pale stranger' for their well-being. The three elders who led them to this place were Oburumankoma, Odapagyan and Oson.

The Old Woman joins the Old Man and they give us important background information about the heroine, Anowa. We learn that she is pretty, and that her beauty has attracted 'sturdy' men to ask for her hand in marriage. Anowa has refused all the offers, though no one knows why. The Old Man describes her as:

> A child of several incarnations,
> She listens to her own tales,
> Laughs at her own jokes and
> Follows her own advice. (p.25)

She has learned to ignore the displeasure of the people in the community, some of whom think her mother, Badua, has spoilt her. Finally, it is hinted that Anowa is a born priestess, but that her mother refused to perform the necessary rituals for that purpose.

Review Questions

When you are answering these questions, always try to find words from the play to support your answers.

1 Why are the Old Man and Old Woman given the name 'The-Mouth-That-Eats-Salt-And-Pepper'?
2 Who do the Old Man and the Old Woman represent?
3 Why do you think the Prologue is important?
4 Find three things which the Old Man tells us about the countryside of Abura, and two things that the Old Woman says about Anowa.
5 Why do the Old Man and the Old Woman enter and leave the stage in opposite directions?

Exercises

1 In one short paragraph on each of them, summarise what the Old Man and the Old Woman tell the audience.

2 Briefly describe the differences between the Old Man and the Old Woman.

Activity

Act the roles of the Old Man and the Old Woman, remembering how they have been described by the author. Choose what you think are the most important lines, and learn them.

Phase One

In Yebi

[Lower Stage. Early evening village noises, for example, the pounding of fufu or millet, a goat bleats loudly, a woman calls her child, etc. ANOWA *enters from lower right, carrying an empty water-pot. She walks to the centre of the lower stage, stops and looks behind her. Then she overturns the water-pot and sits on it facing the audience. She is wearing her cloth wrapped around her. The upper part of her breasts are visible, and also all of her legs. She is slim and slight of build. She turns her face momentarily towards lower left. During a moment when she is looking at her feet,* KOFI AKO *enters from the lower right. He is a tall, broad, young man, and very good-looking. The village noises die down.*

He is in work clothes and carrying a fish trap and a bundle of baits. He steals quietly up to her and cries, 'Hei!' She is startled but regains her composure immediately. They smile at each other. Just then, a WOMAN *comes in from the lower left, carrying a wooden tray which is filled with farm produce – cassava, yam, plantain, pepper, tomatoes, etc. Close behind her is a* MAN, *presumably her husband, also in work-clothes, with a gun on his shoulder and a machet under his arm. They pass by* ANOWA *and* KOFI *and walk on towards lower right. The woman turns round at every step to stare at the boy and girl who continue looking shyly at each other. Finally, the* WOMAN *misses a step or kicks against the block of wood. She falls, her tray crashing down.*

ANOWA *and* KOFI *burst into loud uncontrollable laughter. Assisted by her* MAN, *the* WOMAN *begins to collect her things together. Having got her load back on her head, she disappears, followed by her* MAN. *Meanwhile,* ANOWA *and* KOFI *continue laughing and go on doing so a little while after the lights have been removed from them.*

Upper Stage. The courtyard of Maami BADUA *and Papa* OSAM*'s cottage. Village noises as in previous scene. Standing in the centre* *is an earthen hearth with tripod cooking pot. There are a couple of small household stools standing around. By the right wall is a lie-in chair which belongs exclusively to Papa* OSAM. *Whenever he sits down, he sits in this. By the chair is a small table. The Lower Stage here represents a section of a village side street from which there is an open entrance into the courtyard. In the background, upper left and upper right, are doors connecting the courtyard to the inner rooms of the house.*

In the pot something is cooking which throughout the scene Maami BADUA *will go and stir. By the hearth is a small vessel into which she puts the ladle after each stirring.*

BADUA *enters from upper right, goes to the hearth, picks up the ladle and stirs the soup. She is talking loudly to herself.*]

BADUA: Any mother would be concerned if her daughter refused to get married six years after her puberty. If I do not worry about this, what shall I worry about?

[OSAM *enters from upper left smoking his pipe.*]

Besides, a woman is not a stone but a human being; she grows.

OSAM: Woman, [BADUA *turns to look at him*] that does not mean you should break my ears with your complaints. [*He looks very composed.*]

BADUA: What did you say, Osam?

OSAM: I say you complain too much.

[*He goes to occupy the lie-in chair, and exclaims, 'Ah!' with satisfaction.*]

BADUA: [*Seriously*] Are you trying to send me insane?

OSAM: Will that shut you up?

BADUA: Kofi Sam! [*Now she really is angry.*]

OSAM: Yes, my wife.

[BADUA *breathes audibly with exasperation. She begins pacing up and down the courtyard, with the ladle in her hand.*]

BADUA: [*Moving quickly up to* OSAM] So it is nothing at a—a—l—l [*stretching the utterance of the last word*] to you that your child is not married and goes round wild, making everyone talk about her?

OSAM: Which is your headache, that she is not yet married, or that she is wild?

BADUA: Hmm!

OSAM: You know that I am a man and getting daughters married is not one of my duties. Getting them born, aha! But not finding them husbands.

BADUA: Hmm! [*Paces up and down.*]

OSAM: And may the ancestral spirits help me, but what man would I order from the heavens to please the difficult eye of my daughter Anowa?

BADUA: Hmm! [*She goes and stirs the soup and this time remembers to put the ladle down. She stands musing by the hearth.*]

OSAM: As for her wildness, what do you want me to say again about that? I have always asked you to apprentice her to a priestess to quieten her down. But …

[*Roused again,* BADUA *moves quickly back to where he is and meanwhile, corks both her ears with two fingers and shakes her head to make sure he notices what she is doing.*]

OSAM: [*Chuckles*] Hmm, play children's games with me, my wife. One day you will click your fingers with regret that you did not listen to me.

BADUA: [*She removes her fingers from her ears*] I have said it and I will say it again and again and again! I am not going to turn my only daughter into a dancer priestess.

OSAM: What is wrong with priestesses?

BADUA: I don't say there is anything wrong with them.

OSAM: Did you not consult them over and over again when you could not get a single child from your womb to live beyond one day?

BADUA: [*Reflectively*] O yes. I respect them, I honour them … I fear them. Yes, my husband, I fear them. But my only daughter shall not be a priestess.

OSAM: They have so much glory and dignity …

BADUA: But in the end, they are not people. They become too

much like the gods they interpret. [*As she enumerates the attributes of priesthood, her voice grows hysterical and her face terror-stricken.* OSAM *removes his pipe, and stares at her, his mouth open with amazement.*]
They counsel with spirits;
They read into other men's souls;
They swallow dogs' eyes jump fires
Drink goats' blood
Sheep milk
Without flinching
Or vomiting
They do not feel
As you or I,
They have no shame.

[*She relaxes, and* OSAM *does too, the latter sighing audibly.* BADUA *continues, her face slightly turned away from both her husband and the audience.*]

BADUA: I want my child
To be a human woman
Marry a man,
Tend a farm
And be happy to see her
Peppers and her onions grow.
A woman like her
Should bear children
Many children,
So she can afford to have
One or two die.
Should she not take
Her place at meetings
Among the men and women of the clan?
And sit on my chair when
I am gone? And a captainship in the army,
Should not be beyond her
When the time is ripe!

[OSAM *nods his head and exclaims, 'Oh … oh!'*]

BADUA: But a priestess lives too much in her own and other people's minds, my husband.
OSAM: [*Sighing again*] My wife, people with better vision than yours or mine have seen that Anowa is not like you or me. And a prophet with a locked mouth is neither a prophet nor a man. Besides, the yam that will burn, shall burn, boiled or roasted.
BADUA: [*She picks up the ladle but does not stir the pot. She throws her arms about.*] Since you want to see Nkomfo and Nsofo, seers and dancers ...
ANOWA: [*From the distance*] Mother!
BADUA: That is her coming.
ANOWA: Father!
OSAM: O yes. Well let us keep quiet about her affairs then. You know what heart lies in her chest.
ANOWA: Mother, Father ... Father, Mother ... Mother ...

[OSAM *jumps up and, confused, he and* BADUA *keep bumping into each other as each moves without knowing why or where he or she is moving.* BADUA *still has the ladle in her hands.*]

BADUA: Why do you keep hitting at me?
ANOWA: Mother!
OSAM: Sorry, I did not mean to. But you watch your step too.
ANOWA: Father!
OSAM: And where is she?

[ANOWA *runs in, lower right, with her empty water-pot.*]

BADUA: *Hei.* Why do you frighten me so? And where is the water?
ANOWA: O Mother. [*She stops running and stays on the lower stage.*]
OSAM: What is it?
ANOWA: [*Her eyes swerving from the face of one to the other*] O Father!
OSAM: Say whatever you have got to say and stop behaving like a child.
BADUA: Calling us from the street!
OSAM: What have you got to tell us that couldn't wait until you reached here?

ANOWA: O Father.

BADUA: And look at her. See here, it is time you realised you have grown up.

ANOWA: Mother ... [*Moving a step or two forward.*]

BADUA: And now what is it? Besides, where is the water? I am sure this household will go to bed to count the beams tonight since there is no water to cook with.

ANOWA: Mother, Father, I have met the man I want to marry.

BADUA: What is she saying?

ANOWA: I say I have found the man I would like to marry.

OSAM:
BADUA: } Eh?

[*Long pause during which* BADUA *stares at* ANOWA *with her head tilted to one side.*]

ANOWA: Kofi Ako asked me to marry him and I said I will, too.

BADUA: Eh?

OSAM: Eh?

BADUA: Eh?

OSAM: Eh?

BADUA: Eh?

OSAM:
BADUA: } Eh—eh!

[*Light dies on all three and comes on again almost immediately.* OSAM is *sitting in his chair.* ANOWA *hovers around and she has a chewing-stick in her mouth with which she scrapes her teeth when she is not speaking.* BADUA *is sitting by the hearth doing nothing.*]

ANOWA: Mother, you have been at me for a long time to get married. And now that I have found someone I like very much ...

BADUA: Anowa, shut up. Shut up! Push your tongue into your mouth and close it. Shut up because I never counted Kofi Ako among my sons-in-law. Anowa, why Kofi Ako? Of all the mothers that are here in Yebi, should I be the one whose daughter would want to marry this fool, this good-for-nothing cassava-man, this watery male of all watery males? This-I-am-the-handsome-one-with-a-stick-between-my-teeth-in-the-market-place … This … this …

ANOWA: O Mother …

BADUA: [*Quietly*] I say Anowa, why did you not wait for a day when I was cooking *banku* and your father was drinking palm-wine in the market place with his friends? When you could have snatched the ladle from my hands and hit me with it and taken your father's wine from his hands and thrown it into his face? Anowa, why did you not wait for a day like that, since you want to behave like the girl in the folk tale?

ANOWA: But what are you talking about, Mother?

BADUA: And you, Kobina Sam, will you not say anything?

OSAM: Abena Badua, leave me out of this. You know that if I so much as whisper anything to do with Anowa, you and your brothers and your uncles will tell me to go and straighten out the lives of my nieces. This is your family drum; beat it, my wife.

BADUA: I did not ask you for riddles.

OSAM: Mm … just remember I was smoking my pipe.

BADUA: If you had been any other father, you would have known what to do and what not to do.

OSAM: Perhaps; but that does not mean I would have *done* anything. The way you used to talk, I thought if Anowa came to tell you she was going to get married to Kweku Ananse, or indeed the devil himself, you would spread rich cloth before her to walk on. And probably sacrifice an elephant.

BADUA: And do you not know what this Kofi Ako is like?

ANOWA: What is he like?

BADUA: My lady, I have not asked you a question. [ANOWA *retires into sullenness. She scrapes her teeth noisily.*]

OSAM: How would I know what he is like? Does he not come from Nsona House? And is not that one of the best Houses that are here in Yebi? Has he an ancestor who unclothed himself to nakedness, had the Unmentionable, killed himself or another man?

BADUA: And if all that there is to a young man is that his

family has an unspoiled name, then what kind of a man is he? Are he and his wife going to feed on stones when he will not put a blow into a thicket or at least learn a trade?

OSAM: Anyway, I said long ago that I was removing my mouth from my daughter Anowa's marriage. Did I not say that? She would not allow herself to be married to any man who came to ask for her hand from us and of whom we approved. Did you not know then that when she chose a man, it might be one of whom we would disapprove?

BADUA: But why should she want to do a thing like that?

OSAM: My wife, do remember I am a man, the son of a woman who also has five sisters. It is a long time since I gave up trying to understand the human female. Besides, if you think well of it, I am not the one to decide finally whom Anowa can marry. Her uncle, your brother, is there, is he not? You'd better consult him. Because I know your family: they will say I deliberately married Anowa to a fool to spite them.

ANOWA: Father, Kofi Ako is not a fool.

OSAM: My daughter, please forgive me, I am sure you know him very well. And it was only by way of speaking. Kwame! Kwame! I thought the boy was around somewhere. [*Moves towards lower stage and looks around.*]

BADUA: What are you calling him here for?

OSAM: To go and call us her uncle and your brother.

BADUA: Could we not have waited until this evening or dawn tomorrow?

OSAM: For what shall we wait for the dawn?

BADUA: To settle the case.

OSAM: What case? Who says I want to settle cases? If there is any case to settle, that is between you and your people. It is not everything one chooses to forget, Badua. Certainly, I remember what happened in connection with Anowa's dancing. That is, if you don't. Did they not say in the end that it was I who had prevented her from going into apprenticeship with a priestess?

[*Light dies on them and comes on a little later.* ANOWA *is seen dressed in a two-piece cloth. She darts in and out of upper right, with very quick movements. She is packing her belongings into a little basket. Every now and then, she pauses, looks at her mother and sucks her teeth.* BADUA *complains as before, but this time tearfully.* OSAM *is lying in his chair smoking.*]

BADUA: I am in disgrace so suck your teeth at me. [*Silence*] Other women certainly have happier tales to tell about motherhood. [*Silence*] I think I am just an unlucky woman.

ANOWA: Mother, I do not know what is wrong with you.

BADUA: And how would you know what is wrong with me? Look here Anowa, marriage is like a piece of cloth ...

ANOWA: I like mine and it is none of your business.

BADUA: And like cloth, its beauty passes with wear and tear.

ANOWA: I do not care, Mother. Have I not told you that this is to be my marriage and not yours?

BADUA: My marriage! Why should it be my daughter who would want to marry that good-for-nothing cassava-man?

ANOWA: He is mine and I like him.

BADUA: If you like him, do like him. The men of his house do not make good husbands; ask older women who are married to Nsona man.

OSAM: You know what you are saying is not true. Indeed from the beginning of time Nsona men have been known to make the best of husbands. [BADUA *glares at him.*]

ANOWA: That does not even worry me and it should not worry you, Mother.

BADUA: It's up to you my mistress who knows everything. But remember, my lady – when I am too old to move, I shall still be sitting by these walls waiting for you to come back with your rags and nakedness.

ANOWA: You do not have to wait because we shall not be coming back here to Yebi. Not for a long long time, Mother, not for a long long time.

BADUA: Of course, if I were you I wouldn't want to come back with my shame either.

ANOWA: You will be surprised to know that I am going to help him do something with his life.

BADUA: A—a—h, I wish I could turn into a bird and come and stand on your roof-top watching you make something of that husband of yours. What was he able to make of the plantation of palm-trees his grandfather gave him? And the virgin land his uncles gave him, what did he do with that?

ANOWA: Please, Mother, remove your witch's mouth from our marriage.

[OSAM *jumps up and from now on hovers between the two, trying to make peace.*]

OSAM: *Hei* Anowa, what is wrong with you? Are you mad? How can you speak like that to your mother?

ANOWA: But Father, Mother does not treat me like her daughter.

BADUA: And so you call me a witch? The thing is, I wish I were a witch so that I could protect you from your folly.

ANOWA: I do not need your protection, Mother.

OSAM: The spirits of my fathers! Anowa, what daughter talks like this to her mother?

ANOWA: But Father, what mother talks to her daughter the way Mother talks to me? And now, Mother, I am going, so take your witchery to eat in the sea.

OSAM: *Ei* Anowa?

BADUA: Thank you my daughter. [BADUA *and* ANOWA *try to jump on each other.* BADUA *attempts to hit* ANOWA *but* OSAM *quickly intervenes.*]

OSAM: What has come over this household? Tell me what has come over this household? And you too Badua. What has come over you?

BADUA: You leave me alone, Osam. Why don't you speak to Anowa? She is your daughter, I am not.

OSAM: Well, she is not mature.

BADUA: That one makes me laugh. Who is not mature? Has she not been mature enough to divine me out and discover I am a witch? Did she not choose her husband single-handed? And isn't she leaving home to make a better success of her marriage?

OSAM: Anowa, have you made up your mind to leave?

ANOWA: But Father, Mother is driving me away.

BADUA: Who is driving you away?

ANOWA: You! Who does not know here in Yebi that from the day I came to tell you that Kofi and I were getting married you have been drumming into my ears what a disgrace this marriage is going to be for you? Didn't you say that your friends were laughing at you? And they were saying that very soon I shall be sharing your clothes because my husband will never buy me any? Father, I am leaving this place.

[*She picks up her basket, puts it on her head and moves down towards lower left.*]

BADUA: Yes, go.

ANOWA: I am on my way, Mother.

OSAM: And where is your husband?

ANOWA: I am going to look for him.

OSAM: Anowa, stop! [*But* ANOWA *behaves as if she has not heard him.*] Anowa, you must not leave in this manner.

BADUA: Let her go. And may she walk well.

ANOWA: Mother, I shall walk so well that I will not find my feet back here again.

[*She exits lower left.* OSAM *spits with disdain, then stares at* BADUA *for a long time. She slowly bows her head in the folds of her cloth and begins to weep quietly as the lights die on them. Enter* THE-MOUTH-THAT-EATS-SALT-AND-PEPPER.]

OLD WOMAN: *Hei, hei, hei!* And what do the children of today want? Eh, what would the children of today have us do? Parenthood was always a very expensive affair. But it seems that now there is no man or woman created in nature who is endowed with enough powers to be a mother or a father.

[OLD MAN *enters and walks up to the middle of the lower stage passing* OLD WOMAN *on the way.*]

Listen, listen. The days when children obeyed their elders have run out. If you tell a child to go forward, he will surely step backwards. And if you asked him to move back a pace, he would run ten leagues.

OLD MAN: But what makes your heart race itself in anger so? What disturbs you? Some of us feel that the best way to sharpen a knife is not to whet one side of it only. And neither can you solve a riddle by considering only one end of it. We know too well how difficult children of today are. But who begot them? Is a man a father for sleeping with a woman and making her pregnant? And does bearing the child after nine months make her a mother? Or is she the best potter who knows her clay and how it breathes?

OLD WOMAN: Are you saying that the good parent would not tell his child what should and should not be done?

OLD MAN: How can I say a thing like that?

OLD WOMAN: And must we lie down and have our children play jumping games on our bellies if this is what they want? [*She spits.*]

OLD MAN: Oh no. No one in his rightful mind would say that babies should be free to do what they please. But Abena Badua should have known that Anowa wanted to be something else which she herself had not been ... They say from a very small age, she had the hot eyes and nimble feet of one born to dance for the gods.

OLD WOMAN: Hmm. Our ears are breaking with that one. Who heard the Creator tell Anowa what she was coming to do with her life here? And is that why, after all her 'I don't like this' and 'I don't like that', she has gone and married Kofi Ako?

OLD MAN: Tell me what is wrong in that?

OLD WOMAN: Certainly. Some of us thought she had ordered a completely new man from the heavens.

OLD MAN: Are people angry because she chose her own husband; or is there something wrong with the boy?

OLD WOMAN: As for that Kofi Ako, they say he combs his hair too often and stays too long at the Nteh games.

OLD MAN: Who judges a man of name by his humble beginnings?

OLD WOMAN: Don't ask me. They say Badua does not want him for a son-in-law.

OLD MAN: She should thank her god that Anowa has decided to settle down at all. But then, we all talk too much about those two. And yet this is not the first time since the world began that a man and a woman have decided to be together against the advice of grey-haired crows.

OLD WOMAN: What foolish words! Some people babble as though they borrowed their grey hairs and did not grow them on their own heads! Badua should have told her daughter that the infant which tries its milk teeth on every bone and stone, grows up with nothing to eat dried meat with. [*She exits noisily.*]

OLD MAN: I'm certainly a foolish old man. But I think there is no need to behave as though Kofi Ako and Anowa have brought an evil concoction here. Perhaps it is good for them that they have left Yebi to go and try to make their lives somewhere else.

[*As lights go out, a blending of the* atentenben *with any ordinary drum.*]

Notes

Summary

Phase One begins in the village of Yebi. It is early evening and people are busy cooking their evening meals. Others are just returning from their farms. Some are fetching water to their houses. The setting is part of the village street near the courtyard of Anowa's home. The two main characters are introduced, one after the other. The first to appear is Anowa, who has been sent to go and fetch a pot of water. The second is Kofi Ako who is just returning home from fishing. Anowa shows that she really admires Kofi Ako. We see that they like each other, as 'They smile at each other' and 'continue looking shyly at each other' (p.29). Their relationship is so surprising to other people that a woman carrying farm produce stares at them so hard that she misses a step and falls over.

The scene then shifts to the courtyard of Anowa's parents, Papa Osam and Maami Badua. It is time for the preparation of their evening meal. Here, Badua expresses worry because Anowa has refused to get married, even though she is now a grown-up person. Osam, however, does not seem worried. We learn that Osam has often suggested that Anowa's wild behaviour could be quietened down if they sent her to train to be a priestess. Badua, however, has always been strongly against this idea, even though she consulted the priestesses over and over again before she had this only daughter. She honours, respects and fears the priestesses, but wants Anowa to have a life as a 'human woman' (pp.31–32).

Just then Anowa rushes back home with the empty water pot, and announces to the amazement of her parents that she has now met the man she wants to marry. Badua and Osam are surprised, and Badua is angry to hear that the man is Kofi Ako, whom she describes as:

> … this fool, this good-for-nothing cassava-man, this watery male of all watery males … (pp.34–35)

However, Osam, the father, does not agree with Badua. He says:

> How would I know what he is like? Does he not come from Nsona House? And is not that one of the best Houses that are here in Yebi? Has he an ancestor who unclothed himself to nakedness, had the Unmentionable, killed himself or another man? (p.35)

He is keen to distance himself from matters involving his daughter.

In the next scene we see Anowa and her mother exchanging bitter words. Anowa shows complete disrespect, arrogance, disobedience and pride towards her mother. She takes no notice of Badua's advice and suggestions. Her decision to marry Kofi Ako is final. At this point, Badua, whose main worry is that the men of the Nsona House do not make good husbands, gives up and wishes Anowa ill-luck. This pushes Anowa into calling her mother a witch and saying that she will never come back to Yebi.

Finally, the Old Man and the Old Woman express their feelings about the situation. The Old Woman feels that parenthood is difficult and unattractive, since the children of the time are becoming disobedient and wayward. They both feel that Anowa's parents should take part of the blame, since they failed in their duty to give Anowa the spiritual support that she needed. While the Old Woman is bitterly against Anowa's behaviour, the Old Man sees nothing wrong with the relationship between Kofi Ako and Anowa. The marriage has, however, led to much gossiping among the people of the village.

Review Questions

When you are answering these questions, always try to find words from the play to support your answers.

1 What does Anowa come to tell her parents? Describe how she feels.
2 How do the parents react to the news, firstly before, and then after, they know the whole story?
3 Find some of the things that Osam says which show how he feels about Anowa's choice.
4 Is Anowa happy or unhappy when her mother says she does not want her to marry Kofi Ako?
5 What reasons does Badua give for being against the marriage?
6 Describe Anowa's behaviour towards her mother. Find two passages in the play which support your description.
7 Why does Anowa call her mother a witch? Suggest one or two things which you think will happen to Anowa because of this.
8 What does Badua say to Anowa to make her so angry at the end of Phase One? Should Badua have spoken like that? Give your reasons.
9 What is Anowa's reply to her mother? What is the meaning behind it?

Exercises

1 There is **conflict** between Anowa and Badua, and between Badua and Osam. For each of the two conflicts, describe the causes, what happens, and the result.
2 What do you learn in Phase One about the characters of (a) Anowa (b) Badua (c) Osam? Give reasons based on what they say and do in Phase One.

Activity

A Find out about your own extended family. Ask your parents and older family members about your family's history. Give a presentation to the class.
B Take turns in acting short sequences between Anowa and her parents.

Phase Two

On the Highway

[*The road is represented by the lower stage. A dark night. Wind, thunder and lightning.* KOFI AKO *enters from lower left. He is carrying a huge load of monkey skins and other hides. He looks exhausted and he is extremely wet from the rain.*]

KOFI AKO: [*Softly and without turning round*] Anowa. [*Silence*] Anowa, are you coming? [*There is no response from anywhere. Then, frenziedly,*] Anowa, *ei*, Anowa!

ANOWA: [*Also entering from lower left and carrying basket*] O, and what is wrong with you? Why are you so afraid? [KOFI AKO *turns round to look at her.*]

KOFI AKO: [*Breathing loudly with relief*] It is a fearful night.

ANOWA: But you do not have to fear so much for me. Why Kofi, see how your great chest heaves up and down even through the folds of your cloth! [*Laughs.*]

KOFI: You just let it be then. [*She giggles more.*] And I can't see that there is anything to laugh at … Look at the lightning! Shall we sit here in this thicket?

ANOWA: Yes.

[*They move to upper stage, and stay in the central area.* KOFI AKO *puts his own load down with difficulty. He then helps* ANOWA *to unload hers and sits down immediately.*]

ANOWA: *Hei,* you should not have sat down in the mud just like that.

KOFI AKO: As if it matters. Now sit here and move nearer. [*He pulls* ANOWA, *shivering, down by him.*] Anowa, see how you shiver! And yet my tongue cannot match yours. [*Mocking her*] 'I am strong … O… O … It is not heavy. My body is small but I am strong!' *Ei,* Anowa!

ANOWA: But I am strong.

KOFI: We can see that. You know what? Shivering like this,

with all your clothes wet, you look like a chick in a puddle.

ANOWA: And how about you? [*Beginning to rummage through her basket as though looking for something.*]

KOFI AKO: Do you compare yourself to me? See how big I am. [*He bares his chest and spreads out his arms.*]

ANOWA: [*Pretending to be shocked*] Ahhh! And this is why we should fear more of you. You are so tall and so broad. You really look like a huge something. There is too much of you. [*Touching different parts of him*] Anything can get any part of you ... a branch from a falling tree ... a broken splinter, and ow, my mouth is at the dung heap, even lightning ... But I am so little, I can escape things.

KOFI AKO: I was not born to die in any of these ways you mention.

ANOWA: O seasoned Priest, and how was I born to die, that you are so afraid of me?

KOFI AKO: I have no idea about that one. What I know is that if you stay out longer in this weather, you are going to be ill. And I cannot afford to lose you.

ANOWA: You will never lose me.

KOFI AKO: I thank your mouth.

[ANOWA *fishes out a miserable looking packet of food from the basket.*]

ANOWA: Are you hungry? Here is what is left of the food. Oh, but it is so wet. [*She giggles but gives it to him.*]

KOFI AKO: [*He clutches hungrily at the bundle.*] They are good. How about you?

ANOWA: No, I am not hungry.

KOFI AKO: Perhaps you are ill already. [*Begins to wolf the stuff down*] Mm ... This life is not good for a woman. No, not even a woman like you. It is too difficult. It is over two hundred miles to the coast and I wonder how much we have done ...

ANOWA: We are near Atandasu. This means we have only about thirty miles or more to do ...

KOFI AKO: Is that it? Do you know how many days we have been walking?

ANOWA: No, I have not been counting the days. All I know is that we have been on the highway for about two weeks now. [*Fights sleep.*]

KOFI AKO: The ghost of my fathers!

ANOWA: But think of it, if we are not too tired to go a little further, we shall be there tomorrow.

KOFI AKO: Ei, Anowa. You ought to have been born a man.

ANOWA: Kofi.

KOFI AKO: Hmm … hmm?

ANOWA: Why don't you marry another woman? [KOFI AKO *registers alarm.*] At least she could help us. I could find a good one too. [*Throws up her head to think*] Let me see. There is a girl in one of the villages we go to e … h … what is the name?

KOFI AKO: Anowa, please don't go on. You know you are annoying me.

ANOWA: Ah my master, but I don't understand you. You are the only man in this world who has just one wife and swears to keep only her! [*Silence*] Perhaps it is your medicine's taboo?

KOFI AKO: What medicine are you talking about? What taboo?

ANOWA: Ah Kofi, why has your voice gone fearfully down and so quickly?

KOFI AKO: But you are saying something about medicines and taboos which I don't understand. Were you not the same person who said we didn't need anything of that kind?

ANOWA: And if I said that, then it means from now on I must not mention medicines and taboos, not even in jest? Kofi [*Pause*] … what use do you think they will be to us? Who is interested in harming you or me? Two lonely people who are only trying something just because the bowels are not as wise as the mind; but like baby orphans, will shriek for food even while their mother's body is cold with death …

KOFI AKO: Anowa, the man who hates you does not care if you wait in the sun for your clothes to dry before you can go and join the dance.

ANOWA: But who hates us?

KOFI AKO: My wife, you speak as if we left Yebi with the town singing and dancing our praises. Was not everyone saying something unkind about us? Led by your mother? Anowa, we did not run away from home to go mushroom-hunting or fish-trapping.

ANOWA: I heard you, my husband. But I do not want us to be caught up in medicines or any of those things.

KOFI AKO: I too have heard you, my wife. Meanwhile, I am eating all the food …

ANOWA: Set your mouth free. Mine feels as though it could not stand the smell of anything.

KOFI AKO: [*Putting his hand on her forehead*] Anowa, please, don't be ill.

ANOWA: My mother has often told me that, except for the normal gripes and fevers, my body has never known real illness.

KOFI AKO: Ah, but my wife seems to be extraordinary in more things than one. Anowa …

ANOWA: Yes?

KOFI AKO: We do need something to protect us. Even though no one dislikes us enough now to want to destroy us, how about when we begin to do well? Shall we not get hosts of enemies then?

ANOWA: [*Trying to keep voice light*] But my husband, why should we begin to take to our sick-beds now with illnesses that may affect us in our old age? Kofi, I just don't like the idea of using medicines.

KOFI AKO: But there are many things we do in life which we do not like – which we even hate … and we only need a bead or two.

ANOWA: But a shrine has to be worshipped however small its size. And a kind god angered is a thousand times more evil than a mean god unknown. To have a little something to eat and a rag on our back is not a matter to approach a god about.

KOFI AKO: Maybe you feel confident enough to trust yourself in dealing with all the problems of life. I think I am different, my wife.

[*For some time* ANOWA *quietly looks down while he eats.*]

ANOWA: Kofi, that was unkindly said. Because you know that I am already worried about not seeing signs of a baby yet.

KOFI AKO: It is quite clear that neither of us knows too much about these things. [*Pause*] Perhaps it is too early to worry about such a problem. We can consult a more grown-up person, but I know you would not like us to do anything like that.

ANOWA: [*Very loudly*] Listen to what he is saying! Is it the same thing to ask an older person about a woman's womb as it is to contract medicines in pots and potions which would attract good fortune and ward off evil?

KOFI AKO: I swear by everything that it is the same. And Anowa, it is too fearful a night to go screaming into the woods.

ANOWA: That is true.

[*More thunder and lightning.* ANOWA *begins to nod sleepily. Having finished eating,* KOFI *throws the food wrappers into the woods behind him. Then he notices* ANOWA *nodding.*]

KOFI AKO: Anowa, you are very tired. [*Jumping up*] Let me prepare somewhere for you to sleep.

[*Then he goes off-stage by upper right.* ANOWA *goes on nodding. Meanwhile the storm continues convulsively.*]

ANOWA: [*Startled awake by a peal of thunder*] What I am worried about are these things. [*She gropes towards the baskets and begins to feel the skins.*] See how wet they are. Tomorrow, they will be heavier than sheets of rock. And if it continues like this, they will all rot. Creator, [*she looks up*] do as you like, but please, let your sun shine tomorrow so we can dry out these skins. We must stop in the next village to dry them out. Yes, we must stop if the sun comes out.

KOFI AKO: [*Entering with a couple of plantain or banana leaves which he spreads out to form some kind of mat in the centre of lower stage*] To do what?

ANOWA: To dry out the skins. They are so wet.

[KOFI AKO *concentrates on preparing the mat.* ANOWA *starts nodding again.*]

KOFI AKO: Eh? [*He turns round and sees her.*]

ANOWA: [*Mumbling*] The storm has ruined the whole corn field. Every stalk is down.

KOFI AKO: [*Moving with urgency, he picks her up in his arms*] Come Anowa, you are dreaming. Come to sleep. [*Carries her to the leafy bed*] Yes, Anowa, sleep well. Sleep well, and let every corn stalk go down. We shall not return to see the ruin. [*Pacing up and down the length of lower stage*] Sometimes, I do not understand. Wherever we go, people take you for my sister at first. They say they have never heard of a woman who helped her husband so. 'Your wife is good' they say 'for your sisters are the only women you can force to toil like this for you'. They say that however good for licking the back of your hand is, it would never be like your palms. [*Pause*] Perhaps if they knew what I am beginning to know, they would not say so much. And proverbs do not always describe the truth of reality. [*His face acquires new determination.*] Anowa truly has a few strong ideas. But I know she will settle down. [*Addressing the sleeping woman*] Anowa, I shall be the new husband and you the new wife.

[*Now the storm is raging harder, thunder roars and lightning occurs more frequently. He stares at her for some time and then as lights begin to dim, he spreads out his big figure by her. Lights off. Pause.*
When lights come on again, same scene without the leafy bed. The sun is shining and ANOWA *is spreading out skins from the baskets while* KOFI *stands looking on.*
Then ANOWA *holds her nose elaborately. Both of them burst out laughing. He moves in to help her.*]

KOFI AKO: Our noses are certainly suffering.

ANOWA: And yet what can we do? Without them, where would we stand?

KOFI AKO: Nowhere indeed.

ANOWA: [*Looking into one of the baskets and picking it up*] About two of them in here are too rotten to do anything with. [*She makes a movement of wiping sweat off her face, then yawns.*]

KOFI AKO: Come out of the sun. [*He takes the basket from her and places it away from them.*] Come, let's sit down in the shade. [*They go and sit near one end of the lower stage.*]

ANOWA: [*Breathing audibly*] Did your friend the doctor tell you what is wrong with me?

KOFI AKO: Yes.

ANOWA: What did he say?

KOFI AKO: I should have asked him whether I'm to let you know or not.

ANOWA: Ho! I think you can tell me, because he would not have forgotten to warn you, if he thought I should not know.

KOFI AKO: [*Quietly and with a frown*] He says there is nothing wrong with you.

ANOWA: Then why … ?

KOFI AKO: Let me finish. He says there is nothing wrong with your womb. But your soul is too restless. You always seem to be looking for things; and that prevents your blood from settling.

ANOWA: Oh!

KOFI AKO: Anowa, are you unhappy. Do I make you unhappy?

ANOWA: [*With surprise*] No.

KOFI AKO: Perhaps this work is too much for you.

ANOWA: No. I think I have always been like that.

KOFI AKO: [*Alarmed*] Like what?

ANOWA: I don't know. I can't describe it.

KOFI AKO: Maybe you should stop coming on the roads.

ANOWA: [*Alarmed*] No. Why?

KOFI AKO: Why not?

ANOWA: I like this work. I like being on the roads.

KOFI AKO: My wife, sometimes you talk strangely. I don't see what is so pleasing on these highways. The storms? The wild animals or bad men that we often meet?

ANOWA: There are worse things in villages and towns.

KOFI AKO: Listen to her! Something tells me [*he stands up*] it might be better if you stayed at home. Indeed I have been thinking that may be I should eh … eh …

ANOWA: My husband, I am listening to you.

KOFI AKO: You remember, you were telling me to marry another woman to help us?

ANOWA: Yes.

KOFI AKO: Hmm, I don't want to marry again. Not yet. But I think … I think … that perhaps …

ANOWA: *Eheh!*

KOFI AKO: I think the time has come for us to think of looking for one or two men to help us.

ANOWA: What men?

KOFI AKO: I hear they are not expensive … and if …

ANOWA: [*Getting up so slowly that every movement of her body corresponds to syllables or words in her next speech*] My husband! Am I hear-ing you right? Have we risen so high? [*Corking her ears*] Kofi Ako, do not let me hear these words again.

KOFI AKO: [*Mimicking her*] 'Do not let me hear these words again.' Anowa, do you think I am your son?

ANOWA: I do not care. We shall not buy men.

KOFI AKO: Anowa, look here. You are not always going to have it your way. Who are you to tell me what I must do or not do?

ANOWA: Kofi, I am not telling what you must do or not do … We were two when we left Yebi. We have been together all this time and at the end of these two years, we may not be able to say yet that we are the richest people in the world but we certainly are not starving.

KOFI AKO: And so?

ANOWA: Ah, is there any need then to go behaving as though we are richer than we are?

KOFI AKO: What do you want to say? I am not buying these men to come and carry me. They are coming to help us in our work.

ANOWA: We do not need them.

KOFI AKO: If you don't, I do. Besides you are only talking like a woman.

ANOWA: And please, how does a woman talk? I had as much a mouth in the idea of beginning this trade as you had. And as much head!

KOFI AKO: And I am getting tired now. 'You shall not consult a priest … you shall marry again … we do not need medicines …' Anowa, listen. Now here is something I am going to do whether you like it or not. I do not even understand why you want to make so much noise about something like this. What is wrong with buying one or two people to help us? They are cheap … [*Pause.* ANOWA *walks around in great agitation.* KOFI AKO *continues in a strangely loud voice.*] Everyone does it … does not everyone do it? And things would be easier for us. We shall not be alone … Now you have decided to say nothing, eh? Anowa, who told you that buying men is wrong? You know what? I like you and the way you are different. But Anowa, sometimes, you are too different. [ANOWA *walks away from him.*] I know I could not have started without you, but after all, we all know you are a woman and I am the man.

ANOWA: And tell me, when did I enter into a discussion with you about that? I shall not feel happy with slaves around … Kofi, no man made a slave of his friend and came to much himself. It is wrong. It is evil.

KOFI AKO: [*Showing alarm*] *Hei,* where did you get these ideas from? Who told you all this?

ANOWA: Are there never things which one can think out for oneself?

KOFI AKO: Yes, so now you are saying I am a fool?

ANOWA: [*Collapsing*] O the gods of my fathers!

KOFI AKO: What shall the gods of your fathers do for you? I know you think you are the wise one of the two of us.

ANOWA: Kofi, are you saying all this just so I will take a knife and go cut my throat?

KOFI AKO: Am I lying?

ANOWA: When and where and what did I do to give you this idea?

KOFI AKO: This is the way you have always behaved.

ANOWA: [*Her voice going falsetto*] Kofi! Kofi! [*He sits down by her.*] Hmm! Kofi, we shouldn't quarrel.

KOFI AKO: No, we should not.

[*The lights die on them and come up in a little while, on the upper stage. It is the courtyard of* BADUA's *and* OSAM's *cottage. It is early evening. Village noises.* OSAM *and* BADUA *are having their evening meal.* OSAM *is sitting in the lie-in chair, his food before him. He swallows a morsel.* BADUA's *food is on her lap. She is not eating. Presently she puts it down and gets up noisily. She turns right, she turns left. She begins to move around aimlessly, speaking at the same time.*]

BADUA: I haven't heard the like of this before. A human being, and a woman too, preferring to remain a stranger in other peoples' lands?

OSAM: [*Looking up from his meal*] Sit down, sit down. Sit down, and eat your food. [*Shamefaced,* BADUA *sits down.*] Hmmm, I was telling you. This child of yours ... hm ... She was never even a child in the way a child must be a child.

BADUA: [*Turning round to face him*] And how must a child be a child?

OSAM: *Ei*, are you now asking me? I thought this is what you too have known all along. Ah, Nana, I beg you. Maybe that was not well said. [*Pause*] But I must say it has happened before us all. Has it not? Walked out of that door, she did, how long ago is that?

BADUA: Hmmm!

OSAM: ... and has never been back since. I have always feared her.

BADUA: [*Shocked*] You have always feared her? And is that a good thing to say about your own bowel-begotten child? If you fear her, then what do other people do? And if other people fear her then since a crab never fathers a bird, in their eyes, who are you yourself? After all, what has she done? She only went away with her husband and has not been back since.

OSAM: And that, you will agree with me, is very strange.

[*Guessing he might want a helping of the soup, she gets up and goes for his bowl.*]

BADUA: Yes, it is strange, but that does not make me say I fear her.

[*She takes the bowl to the hearth, and returns it to him after she has filled it.*]

OSAM: But don't other women leave their homes to go and marry? And do they stay away forever? Do they not return with their children to the old homestead to attend funerals, pay death debts, return for the feeding of their family stools? And Badua, listen here, if they did not do that, what would homes-and-homes do? Would not the clans break up for lack of people at home? The children of women like Anowa and their children-after-them never find their ways back. They get lost. For they often do not know the names of the founders of their houses … No, they do not know what to tell you if you asked them for just the names of their clans.

BADUA: Anowa has not yet had children.

OSAM: There you are. And is not that too strange? She has not had children. And barrenness is not such a common affliction in your family, is it?

BADUA: No, they have been saying it for a long time around here that she and her husband sold her birth-seeds to acquire their wealth.

OSAM: Of course, women have mouths to talk with. And indeed they open them anyhow and much of the time what comes out is nothing any real man can take seriously. Still, something tells me that this time she has given them cause.

BADUA: O Kofi Sam! [*She returns to her seat and places her bowl on her knee again.*]

OSAM: What have I done? I am not saying that they are right. But it certainly looks as if she and her husband are too busy making money and have no time to find out and cure what is wrong with her womb.

BADUA: Perhaps I should go and look for her.

OSAM: Go and look for her? How? Where? And anyway, who told you she is lost?

BADUA: But she is my child.

OSAM: And so what? Do you think Anowa will forgive you anymore for that? Please, leave her to live her life!

BADUA: Why are you always against me where Anowa is concerned?

OSAM: You have been against me too. Did I not tell you to …

BADUA: – Make her a priestess … make her a priestess … Always. Why? Why did everyone want me to put my only child on the dancing ground? Since you want to see possessed women so much, why didn't you ask your sisters to apprentice their daughters to oracles?

OSAM: [*Very angry*] Don't shout at me, woman! Who comes complaining to me about Anowa? … They say that that would have been to the good of us all. But now – there she is, as they said she might be, wandering … her soul hovering on the outer fringes of life and always searching for something … and I do not know what!

BADUA: [*Quietly*] I don't know what you mean by all this. Who is not searching in life?

OSAM: I know you have just made up your mind never to understand me.

BADUA: [*Bitterly*] Besides, that daughter of ours is doing well, I hear. Yes, for someone whose soul is wandering, our daughter is prospering. Have you heard from the blowing winds how their trade with the white men is growing? And how they are buying men and women?

OSAM: Yes, and also how unhappy she is about those slaves, and how they quarrel from morning till night.

BADUA: So! I didn't know she was a fool too. She thought it is enough just to be headstrong. [*Laughing drily*] Before she walked out that noon-day, she should have waited for me to tell her how to marry a man …

OSAM: Hmm.

BADUA: A good woman does not have a brain or mouth.

OSAM: Hmm. [*He coughs.*]

BADUA: And if there is something wrong with their slaves, why don't they sell them?

OSAM: That is not the problem. They say she just does not like the idea of buying men and women.

BADUA: What foolishness. People like her are not content to have life cheap, they always want it cheaper. Which woman in the land would not wish to be in her place?

OSAM: Anowa is not every woman.

BADUA: *Tchiaa!* And who does she think she is? A goddess? Let me eat my food. [*She goes to sit down and places the food back on her lap.*]

OSAM: And can I have some soup?

BADUA: Yes. [*As she gets up again, the lights die on the courtyard.*]

[*Eight men in a single file carrying skins enter by lower right, move silently up and across the main stage and away lower left.* KOFI AKO *follows closely behind them but stops in the centre of the lower stage. He is better dressed than before. He is carrying what seems to be a ridiculously light load. From offstage,* ANOWA*'s voice heard calling 'Kofi, Kofi.' He stops, she enters from the same direction, dressed as in the last scene although the lapse in time represents years. She is still barefooted. She is carrying nothing but a small stick which she plays with as she talks.*]

KOFI AKO: What is the matter?

ANOWA: Oh I just want you to wait for me.

KOFI AKO: Anowa, you walked faster when you carried loads which were heavier than mine.

ANOWA: Well, you took the load off my head. But don't you complain about my steps. I cannot keep up with you. These days you are always with your men.

KOFI AKO: [*Smiles*] Is that it? You know what? Let us sit down. [*They move to their position of the previous scene. Then, as if he has remembered something, he moves some steps up towards the left and calls*] Boy!

BOY: [*Running in*] Father!

KOFI AKO: Tell the others that you are to sit down and rest a little.

BOY: Is our Mother coming to give us the food?

KOFI AKO: You can share it among yourselves, can you not?

BOY: We can, Father.

KOFI AKO: Then go and tell Yaako to share it up for you.

BOY: [*He leaves.*] Yes, Father.

KOFI AKO: [*Goes back to sit by* ANOWA] I think we should not come again with them. Yaako is very good and honest and he can manage everything.

ANOWA: [*Quietly*] Is that so?

KOFI AKO: I feel so.

ANOWA: [*Quietly*] Yes.

KOFI AKO: Why do you say that so sadly?

ANOWA: Did I say that sadly? Maybe I am sad. And how not? I cannot be happy if I am going to stop working.

KOFI AKO: But why, Anowa?

ANOWA: Men whom Odomankoma creates do not stop working ... yes, they do, but only when they are hit by illness or some misfortune. When their bodies have grown impotent with age.

KOFI AKO: Anowa, the farmer goes home from the farm ...

ANOWA: [*Gets up and starts walking before* KOFI AKO] And the fisherman brings his boat and nets to the shore ...

KOFI AKO: And if you know this already, then why?

ANOWA: They return in the morning.

KOFI AKO: But we have finished doing all that needs to be done by us.

ANOWA: Kofi, one stops wearing a hat only when the head has fallen off.

KOFI AKO: [*Irritably*] Anowa, can one not rest a tired neck?

ANOWA: Are we coming back after some time?

KOFI AKO: No.

ANOWA: What shall we be doing?

KOFI AKO: Nothing. We shall be resting.

ANOWA: How can a human being rest all the time? I cannot.

KOFI AKO: I can.

ANOWA: I shall not know what to do with myself as each day breaks.

KOFI AKO: You will look after the house.

ANOWA: No. I am going to marry you to a woman who shall do that.

KOFI AKO: You will not marry me to any woman. I am not sending you on that errand.

ANOWA: See if I don't. One of these plump Oguaa mulatto women. With a skin as smooth as shea-butter and golden like fresh palm-oil on yam …

KOFI AKO: [*Jumping up and showing undue irritation*] Anowa, stop that!

ANOWA: Stop what?

KOFI AKO: What you are doing!

ANOWA: What am I doing? [*Pause*] *Ei,* master, let your heart lie cool in your chest.

KOFI AKO: Haven't I told you several times not to talk to me about marrying other women?

ANOWA: Hmm, I am quiet. [*Pause*]

KOFI AKO: [*Cooling down*] And if I marry again what will become of you?

ANOWA: Nothing that is unheard of. Ask your friends. What becomes of other women whose husbands have one, two, or more other wives besides themselves?

KOFI AKO: So what you want to be is my mother-wife?

ANOWA: Yes, or your friend or your sister. Have we not enough memories to talk about from our working days until we get tired of them and each other, when we shall sit and wait for our skins to fall off our bones?

KOFI AKO: Your mood is on. [*He stretches his left arm forward and looks at it intently.*]

ANOWA: [*Giggling*] What mood? You are always funny. My nothing is on. It is just that when I throw my eyes into the future, I do not see myself there.

KOFI AKO: This is because you have no children. Women who have children can always see themselves in the future.

ANOWA: Mm … children. It would be good to have them. But it seems I'm not woman enough. And this is another reason why you ought to marry another woman. So she can bear your children. [*Pause*] Mm, I am only a wayfarer, with no belongings either here or there.

KOFI AKO: What? What are you saying? Wayfarer, you? But are you talking about … about slaves … and you … ? But, a wayfarer belongs to other people!

ANOWA: Oh no, not always. One can belong to oneself without belonging to a place. What is the difference between any of your men and me? Except that they are men and I'm a woman? None of us belongs.

KOFI AKO: You are a strange woman, Anowa. Too strange. You never even show much interest in what the oracles say. But you are not at fault; they all say the same thing. Anowa, what makes you so restless? What occupies you?

ANOWA: Nothing. Nothing at all.

KOFI AKO: [*Walking away from her*] Anowa, is it true that you should have been a priestess?

ANOWA: O yes? But how would I know? And where did you hear that from? [*Looking genuinely lost.*]

KOFI AKO: Don't think about that one then. It doesn't matter. Still, there is too much restlessness in you which is frightening. I think maybe you are too lonely with only us men around. [*Pause*] I have decided to procure one or two women, not many. Just one or two, so that you will have companionship of your kind.

ANOWA: [*Almost hysterical*] No, no, no! I don't want them. I don't need them.

KOFI AKO: But why not?

ANOWA: No! I just do not need them. [*Long pause*] People can be very unkind. A wayfarer is a traveller. Therefore, to call someone a wayfarer is a painless way of saying he does not belong. That he has no home, no family, no village, no stool of his own; has no feast days, no holidays, no state, no territory.

KOFI AKO: [*Jumping up, furious*] Shut up, woman, shut up!

ANOWA: Why, what have I done wrong?

KOFI AKO: Do you ask me? Yes, what is wrong with you? If you want to go and get possessed by a god, I beg you go. So that at least I shall know that a supernatural being speaks with your lips … [ANOWA*'s eyes widen with surprise*] I say Anowa, why must you always bring in this …

ANOWA: What?

KOFI AKO: About slaves and all such unpleasant affairs?

ANOWA: They are part of our lives now.

KOFI AKO: [*Shaking his head*] But is it necessary to eat your insides out because of them? [*Then with extreme intensity*] Why are you like this? What evil lies in having bonded men? Perhaps, yes [*getting expansive*] in other lands. Among other less kindly people. A meaner race of men. Men who by other men are worse treated than dogs. But here, have you looked around? Yes. The wayfarer here belongs where he is. Consorts freely with free-born nephews and nieces. Eats out of the same vessel, and drinks so as well. And those who have the brains are more listened to than are babbling nobility. They fight in armies. Where the valiant and well-proven can become a captain just as quickly as anyone. How many wayfarers do we know who have become patriarchs of houses where they used only to serve?

ANOWA: But in all this, they are of account only when there are no free-born people around. And if they fare well among us, it is not so among all peoples. And even here, who knows what strange happenings go on behind doors?

KOFI AKO: [*Irritated beyond words, he seizes and shakes her.*] Anowa, Anowa, where else have you been but here? Why can't you live by what you know, what you see? What do you gain by dreaming up miseries that do not touch you? Just so you can have nightmares?

ANOWA: [*Still cool, she stares at him*] It seems this is how they created me.

KOFI AKO: [*Letting go of her*] Hmm. How sad ... And yet if I gave you two good blows on your cheeks which flashed lightning across your face, all this foolishness would go out of your head. [*To himself*] And what is wrong with me? Any man married to her would have by now beaten her to a pulp, a dough. But I can never lay hands on her ... I cannot even think of marrying another woman. O it is difficult to think through anything. All these strange words! [ANOWA *continues to stare at him.*] Anowa, what is the difference? How is it you can't feel like everybody else does? What is the meaning of this strangeness? Who were you in the spirit world? [*Laughing mirthlessly*] I used to like you very much. I wish I could rid you of what ails you, so I could give you peace. And give myself some. [ANOWA *still only stares at him.*] It is an illness, Anowa. An illness that turns to bile all the good things of here-under-the-sun. Shamelessly, you rake up the dirt of life. You bare our wounds. You are too fond of looking for the common pain and the general wrong.

[ANOWA *manages to look sad. She sighs audibly, then hangs down her head as if ashamed. He looks down at her.*]

Anowa, you are among women my one and only treasure. Beside you, all others look pale and shadowless. I have neither the desire nor wish to marry any other, though we all know I can afford dozens more. But please, bring your mind home. Have joy in our overflowing wealth. Enhance this beauty nature gave you with the best craftsmanship in cloth and stone. Be happy with that which countless women would give their lives to enjoy for a day. Be happy in being my wife and maybe we shall have our own children. Be my glorious wife, Anowa, and the contented mother of my children.

[ANOWA'S *answer is a hard grating laugh that goes on and on even after the lights have gone out on them.*

The lights reappear after a little while. Enter THE-MOUTH-THAT-EATS-SALT-AND-PEPPER. *First,* OLD MAN. *He walks up to the centre of the lower stage, and for a short while, stands still with his head down. Then he raises his head and speaks.*]

OLD MAN: My fellow townsmen. Have you heard what Kofi and Anowa are doing now? They say he is buying men and women as though they were only worth each a handful of the sands on the shore. *Ei,* Anowa and Kofi. Were those not the same who left Yebi like a pair of unwanted strangers? But peace creates forgetfulness and money-making is like a god possessing a priest. He never will leave you, until he has occupied you, wholly changed the order of your being, and seared you through and up and down. Then only would he eventually leave you, but nothing of you except an exhausted wreck, lying prone and wondering who you are. [*Enter* OLD WOMAN] Besides, there must be something unwholesome about making slaves of other men, something that is against the natural state of man and the purity of his worship of the gods. Those who have observed have remarked that every house is ruined where they take in slaves.

As you sit,
They grow
And before you know
Where you are,
They are there,
And you are not.
One or two homes in Abura already show this;
They are spilling over
With gold and silver
And no one knows the uttermost hedges of their lands.
But where are the people
Who are going to sit on these things?
Yes,
It is frightening.
But all at once,
Girl-babies die
And the breasts of women in new motherhood
Run dry.

[OLD WOMAN *tries to get in a word, thumping her stick and coughing.*]

OLD WOMAN: She is a witch,
She is a devil,
She is everything that is evil.

OLD MAN: [*Raising his head and showing interest*] Who?

OLD WOMAN: Who else but that child of Abena Badua?

OLD MAN: And what has she done now?

OLD WOMAN: Have you not heard? [*She is even more excited than ever. And for the rest of the scene makes an exhibition of herself, jumping, raising her stick in the air, coughing etc.*] She thinks the world has not seen the likes of her before. [*Now with feigned concern*] I wonder what a woman eats to produce a child like Anowa. I am sure that such children are not begotten by normal natural processes.

OLD MAN: [*With amused contempt*] But what?

OLD WOMAN: Ah! They issue from cancerous growths, tumours that grow from evil dreams. Yes, and from hard and bony material that the tender organs of ordinary human women are too weak to digest.

OLD MAN: Are you not sure that you are seeing too much in too little?

OLD WOMAN: What are you saying? Am I wrong? What woman is she who thinks she knows better than her husband in all things?

OLD MAN: A good husband would himself want advice from his wife, as the head of a family, a chief, a king, any nobleman has need of an adviser.

OLD WOMAN: But Anowa is too much. She is now against the very man who she selected from so many. She would rather he was poor than prospering. They say she raves hourly against our revered ancestors and sanctions their deeds in high tones. She thinks our forefathers should have waited for her to be born so she could have upbraided them for their misdeeds and shown them what actions of men are virtuous.

OLD MAN: I do not know if I can believe all this you say of the pitiful child. But certainly, it is not too much to think that the heavens might show something to children of a latter day which was hidden from them of old?

[OLD WOMAN *is so flabbergasted at this she opens her mouth wide and turns in the* OLD MAN's *direction while he walks slowly away.*]

OLD WOMAN: [*Closing her mouth in a heavy sigh*] But, people of Yebi, rejoice,

For Kofi Ako has prospered
And he is your son.
Women of Nsona house,
They say Kofi Ako can stand
On his two feet to dress up fifty brides
And without moving a step,
Dress up fifty more.
And where and when did this last happen
But in fables and the days of dim antiquity?
They say Kofi sits fat like a bullfrog in a swamp,
While *that* Anowa daily grows thin,
Her eyes popping out of her head like those of
A hungry toad in a parched grassland.
But she is the one
Who must not be allowed to step on any threshold here!
When was this infant born,
That would teach us all what to do?
Who is she to bring us new rules to live by?
It is good she said she was not coming back to Yebi,
But if she so much as crosses the stream
That lies at the mouth of the road,
We shall show her that
Little babies only cry for food
When hungry,
But do not instruct their elders how to tend a farm:
Besides,
As the sourest yam
Is better than the sweetest guava,
The dumbest man is
Always better than a woman.
Or *he* thinks he is!
And so Kofi shall teach Anowa
He is a man!

[OLD WOMAN *exits coughing and her throat wheezing.*]

Notes

Summary

The action starts on the highway. Kofi Ako and Anowa have left the unfriendliness of their native land. They are making a living elsewhere by trading animal skins. The weather is stormy. It is dark, and there is thunder, lightning and rain. Kofi Ako feels that 'It is a fearful night' (p.44). It seems as if Nature itself is against them, but they are very determined. They show love and support for each other, and are not discouraged, even by having to travel 200 miles. As they pass the night in the bush, they discuss the possibility of seeking spiritual assistance and protection. While Anowa is against the idea, because no medicine is given for free, Kofi Ako thinks it is very necessary.

Perhaps Anowa's major concern is that such medicines, gods or shrines may even prevent her from having her own children.

The next day is sunny. Anowa dries all the wet skins. As they sit together in the shade and talk to each other we learn that Kofi has already consulted a spiritual doctor. Among other things which Kofi at first refuses to disclose, the doctor has said that Anowa's soul is too restless for her to have a child. Kofi wishes that Anowa would stay at home and stop coming on the roads, working. He would rather buy slaves to help them in their trade. Anowa hates the idea of possessing slaves. To her, making slaves of fellow human beings is 'evil' and 'wrong'. Their disagreement almost becomes serious, but they agree that they should not quarrel.

In the next scene, we are back in Yebi, in the courtyard of the cottage of Papa Osam and Maami Badua. It is evening and it is time for their supper. Badua's first worry is how Anowa and her husband can choose to be strangers in other people's lands. Both Osam and Badua think that Anowa and her husband have stayed too long away from home, failing to make their offerings, and to know the founders of their houses. They are lost. Badua's second worry is that Anowa has not yet had children. This is strange because, according to Papa Osam, barrenness is not common in Maami Badua's family. In fact, people have been saying of Anowa that:

> ... she and her husband sold her birth-seeds to acquire their wealth. (p.54)

As a typical African mother, Badua feels like going to look for Anowa. When

Osam asks why, she simply says, 'But she is my child.' (p.55)

Papa Osam, however, attributes Anowa's 'strange' behaviour – the strength of her ideas, her dislike for slavery and her inability to have children – to the fact that Badua did not make her a priestess.

In the next scene we are back on the roads, some years later. Kofi Ako is now very rich. He has purchased more slaves to help them in their trade. This has affected Anowa badly. She is no longer working, but she doesn't want to be a housewife with nothing to do.

She would rather Kofi Ako married another woman who would stay in his house. We notice that while Anowa is bitter about the idea of buying slaves, Kofi Ako is very bitter about the idea of marrying any other woman. They continually misunderstand each other. Kofi Ako now feels that Anowa is too strange and restless, and it is clear that Anowa is no longer happy in her marriage.

At the end of Phase Two, The Old Man and the Old Woman (The-Mouth-That-Eats-Salt-And-Pepper) come to speak to the audience. The Old Man first tells the audience about the situation of Kofi Ako and Anowa. The Old Man does not think that making slaves of other people is wholesome. To him it is:

> … against the natural state of man and the purity of his worship of the gods … every house is ruined where they take in slaves. (p.62)

The Old Woman, on the other hand, says that Anowa is a witch, a devil, and everything that is evil. She thinks Anowa is too strong for her husband. The Old Woman is happy that Kofi Ako, a son of Yebi, has prospered. She talks also about the contrast between him and Anowa, and reminds the audience that Anowa can never return to Yebi.

Review Questions

When you are answering these questions, always try to find words from the play to support your answers.

1 Phase Two starts 'on the highway'. What do you think this means? Why is it important?

2 How would you describe the relationship between Anowa and Kofi Ako at the beginning of this Phase?

3 Why does Kofi Ako suggest that he and Anowa 'need something to protect' themselves (p.47)? What does he mean by 'something'? What is Anowa's feeling about this?

4 Anowa and Kofi Ako seem to be worried over something missing in their marriage. What is it, and how do they react to it? Use their words as much as you can.

5 Badua and Osam appear again in Phase Two. Describe Badua's behaviour and say why she is worried. How does Osam react to Badua's worries?

6 What part is played by the slaves in Phase Two? What do they do? What is their importance to this part of the play?

7 What is the main reason for the conflict between Anowa and Kofi Ako later in Phase Two?

Exercises

1 There is a sharp **contrast** between Kofi Ako and Anowa in their physical appearance and in their characters. Describe the differences which make this contrast. Why has the author done this?

2 Describe the relationship between Anowa and Kofi Ako (pp.56–61) after the scene between Badua and Osam. Compare their relationship now with how it was at the beginning of Phase Two. Which is better, and why?

3 What are the attitudes of the Old Man and the Old Woman to the unhappiness of Anowa and Kofi Ako?

Activities

A Phase Two is divided into three scenes. Give a short account of what happens, and how each character feels, in each of these scenes.

B Act out the scenes, discussing each scene when you have finished it.

Phase Three

The Big House at Oguaa

[*The upper stage is a big central hall. The furniture here is either consciously foreign or else opulent. There are beautiful skins lying on the richly carpeted floor. Other articles include a giant sideboard on which are standing huge decanters, with or without spirits, and big decorative plates. In the central wall is a fireplace and above it, a picture of Queen Victoria unamused. To the left of the Queen is a picture of* KOFI AKO *himself, and, to the right, a large painting of the crow, the totem bird of the Nsona clan. In the centre of the room is a gilded chair with rich-looking cushions, and in front of it, a leopard skin. The lower stage represents here a path leading from the house into the town and outside generally.*

The lights blaze on both lower and upper stages to a tumult which at first is distant but draws nearer and nearer to lower right. First a group of women, any number from four, enter from the right, dancing to no distinct form and with great abandon. Meanwhile they sing, or rather recite.]

He is coming!
Nana is coming,
He is coming,
The master of the earth is coming.
Give way,
O—o— give way!
For the Master of all you see around is coming.
Turn your face, the jealous!
Close your eyes, the envious!
For he is coming,
Nana is coming!

[*They pass on and away lower left, and after them, a lone man comes blowing* KOFI AKO*'s horn to the rhythm of just two lines.*]

Turn your face, the jealous!

Close your eyes, the envious!

[*The* HORNBLOWER *stops on the stage while multitudes enter from the same direction and move away lower left. They are men and women carrying raw materials, skins, copra, crude rubber and kegs of palm oil. Controlling the exportation of the last product has made* KOFI AKO *the richest man, probably, of the whole Guinea Coast. Other men and women are carrying cheap silks and madras cloth, muskets, hurricane lamps, knives and enamel ware.*

KOFI AKO *enters, borne by four brawny men in some kind of a carrier chair, basket or sedan. He is resplendent in brilliant kente or velvet cloth and he is over-flowing with gold jewelry, from the crown on his head to the rings on his toes. He is surrounded by more hailing women and an orchestra of horns and drums. As he passes, he makes the gestures of lordship over the area. The procession goes off, lower left; the* HORNBLOWER *is the last man to leave.*

When the tumult has died down, ANOWA *enters from upper left and sits on one side of the chairs in the central hall. She looks aged and forlorn in her old clothes. She is still bare-footed. She sits quietly for a while, as though waiting for somebody, then she stands up and begins to pace around, speaking to herself.*]

ANOWA: [*As she speaks, she makes childish gestures, especially with her hands, to express all the ideas behind each sentence.*] I remember once. I think I was very young then. Quite young certainly. Perhaps I was eight, or ten. Perhaps I was twelve. My grandmother told me of her travels. She told of the great places she had been to and the wonderful things she had seen. Of the sea that is bigger than any river and boils without being hot. Of huge houses rising to touch the skies, houses whose foundations are wider than the biggest roads I had ever seen. They contained more rooms than were in all the homes I knew put together. Of these houses, I asked: Tell me Nana, who built the houses?
She said:

Why do you want to know?
The pale men.
Who are the pale men?
I asked.
You ask too many questions.
They are the white men.
Who are the white men?
I asked.
A child like you should not ask questions.
They come from far away.
Far away from beyond the horizon.
Nana, what do they look like?
I asked.
Shut up child.
Not like you or me,
She said.
But what do they look like, Nana?
I asked.
Shut up child or your mouth will twist up one day with questions.
Not like you or me?
Yes like you or me,
But different.
What do they look like, Nana?
What devil has entered into you, child?
As if you or I
Were peeled of our skins,
Like a lobster that is boiled or roasted,
Like ... like ... but it is not good
That a child should ask questions.
Nana, why did they build the big houses?
I asked.
I must escape from you, child.
They say they said they built the big houses to keep the slaves.
What is a slave, Nana?
Shut up! It is not good that a child should ask big questions.

A slave is one who is bought and sold.
Where did the white men get the slaves?
I asked.
You frighten me, child.
You must be a witch, child.
They got them from the land.
Did the men of the land sell other men of the land, and women and children to pale men from beyond the horizon who looked like you or me peeled, like lobsters boiled or roasted?
I do not know, child.
You are frightening me, child.
I was not there!
It is too long ago!
No one talks of these things anymore!
All good men and women try to forget;
They have forgotten!
What happened to those who were taken away?
Do people hear from them?
How are they?
Shut up child.
It is too late child.
Sleep well, child.
All good men and women try to forget;
They have forgotten!

[*Pause*]

That night, I woke up screaming hot; my body burning and sweating from a horrible dream. I dreamt that I was a big, big woman. And from my insides were huge holes out of which poured men, women and children. And the sea was boiling hot and steaming. And as it boiled, it threw out many, many giant lobsters, boiled lobsters, each of whom as it fell turned into a man or woman, but keeping its lobster head and claws. And they rushed to where I sat and seized the men and women as they poured out of me, and they tore them apart, and dashed them to the ground and stamped upon them. And from their huge courtyards, the women ground my men and women and children on mountains of stone. But there was never a cry or a murmur; only a bursting, as of a ripe tomato or a swollen pod. And everything went on and on and on. [*Pause*]

I was very ill and did not recover for weeks. When I told my dream, the women of the house were very frightened. They cried and cried and told me not to mention the dream again. For some time, there was talk of apprenticing me to a priestess. I don't know what came of it. But since then, any time there is mention of a slave, I see a woman who is me and a bursting of a ripe tomato or a swollen pod.

[*She now stares straight and sharply at the audience for a long time, and then slowly leaves the stage by upper right. Then suddenly, the voices of an unseen wearied multitude begin to sing 'Swing Low, Sweet Chariot'. The song goes on for a while and stops. Long pause while lights remain on. Then the lights go off on the lower stage only.* GIRL *enters from upper right. She resembles* ANOWA *of a long time ago. She is dressed in a one-piece cloth wrapped around her. She, too, looks like a wild one, and she is carrying a broom and a duster with which she immediately begins to dust and sweep. Then suddenly she stops and just stands dreamily. Meanwhile,* BOY *enters from upper right and quietly steals behind her and cries 'Hei!' She is startled.*]

GIRL: [*Turning round to face* BOY] How you frightened me.

BOY: Have you just started working in here? And why were you standing there like that?

GIRL: That is none of your business.

BOY: I don't know what is happening in this house. I am sure there are more people here than in Oguaa town. Yet nothing gets done.

GIRL: But you!

BOY: I what? Is this the hour you were instructed to come and clean the place up?

GIRL: Well, that is not my fault.

BOY: What is not your fault? Look at those arms. I wonder what they could do even if you were not so lazy. Listen, today is Friday and Father is going to come in here. And don't stand there staring at me.

GIRL: And anyway, are you the new overseer? Why don't you leave me alone?

BOY: [*Playfully pulling her nose*] I won't!

GIRL: You! [*She raises her arm to hit him, and causes one of the decorative plates to fall. It breaks.* BOY *is furious.*]

BOY: God, what is wrong with you? Look at what you've done!

GIRL: Well, it's broken, isn't it? I wouldn't fuss so much if I were you.

BOY: Doesn't anything bother you?

GIRL: Not much. Certainly not this plate.

[*She bends down to pick up the pieces. Then she stands up again.*]

This mistress will not miss it. After all, she has no time these days for things like plates.

BOY: You are mad, that's all. I thought she said we should always call her 'Mother' and the master 'Father'.

GIRL: [*Giggling*] Some Mother and Father, heh!

BOY: I don't think I have said anything for you to laugh at.

GIRL: You are being very unfair. You know I like both of them very much. [*Earnestly*] I wish I really was their child … born to them. [*She pouts.*] As for her too.

BOY: What has happened now?

GIRL: Nothing. Now she flits about like a ghost, talking to herself. [*They stop and listen.* BOY *moves up to upper left and peeps.*] Is she coming?

BOY: [*Not turning round*] No. [*Then he moves back towards* GIRL.]

GIRL: Listen, they were saying at the fish-kilns that she went and stared at Takoa's baby so hard that the baby is having convulsions …

BOY: [*Shocked*] Ow!

GIRL: Takoa is certainly telling everyone that Mistress, I mean Mother, is swallowing the baby because she is a witch.

BOY: Hei! [*The* GIRL *is startled. The* BOY *moves closer to face her and begins hitting her lips with the fourth finger of his right hand.*] Don't let me catch you repeating any of the things those awful women say about Mother.

GIRL: Yes, grandfather.

BOY: And you, where did you hear all these things from?

GIRL: [*Petulantly*] I said at the kilns [*throwing her mouth at him*]. Or are you deaf?

BOY: I am not deaf but people in this house talk too much.

GIRL: It is because of this new affair. And the truth is, she herself talks more about it than anyone else. Whenever she thinks she is alone anywhere, she begins 'O my husband, what have I done, what have I done?' [*She imitates someone puzzled and asks the questions with her hands. Then she giggles.*]

BOY: Don't laugh. Have you seen how you yourself will end? [*He picks her duster up and begins to dust around.*]

GIRL: *Ei*, don't turn wise on me. [*Noticing him working*] Good. You should dust since you're keeping me from doing my work …

BOY: Huh! … And are you not a woman too?

GIRL: [*Promptly and loudly*] And if I am? [*She lets fall the broom, and looks up for some time without saying anything.*]

BOY: I did not say you can now rest.

GIRL: [*Quietly and to herself*] If I had more money than I knew what to do with, but not a single child, I should be unhappy. If my man refused to talk to me, I should soon start talking to myself; if he would not come to my room or allow me in his, I should pace around in the night. [*She now turns to look at the* BOY.] And after killing myself for him, he said to me one day, go away, and would not tell me why, I should then die of surprise!

BOY: People do not die of surprise.

GIRL: See if I do not.

BOY: [*Whispering*] What do you think is going to happen now?

GIRL: Do I know? All I know is that if she goes away, I shall run away too.

BOY: I shall come with you.

GIRL: [*Coyly*] Not if you would be scolding me all the time …
BOY: [*Drawing near her and trying to touch her breasts*] No, I shall not.

[*The* GIRL *hits his hand away. They stand still for a moment. Then they resume working with vigour. The* BOY *begins to whistle some tune.*]

GIRL: And the way she carries on with everyone here …
BOY: Playing with us as though we were her kinsmen?
GIRL: Yes; perhaps that is why the master wants to send her away.
BOY: Maybe; and she certainly is more poorly dressed than some of us.
GIRL: Yes, that is another thing. Can't she do something about herself?
BOY: What, for instance?
GIRL: Ho, does she not see her friends, how they go around? All those new and fashionable nkabasroto and bubas? The sleeves blowing out in the wind, the full pointed shoes and the stockings …
BOY: Of course, that is what *you* would like …
GIRL: Why, if I were her, what would I not do,
what would I not have?
As much as my eye will fancy
and the best my heart desires?

[*She forgets she should be working and lets fall the broom. Her eyes light up with joyful expectation and she acts out her dream to the amazed fascination of* BOY.]

Nkente to sit in for all my work days.
Velvets for visiting. Silks for Sundays.

[ANOWA *enters unnoticed and stands at the door. She looks as she did in the last scene, but wizened now and shabby. She is wearing her old cloth and is barefooted. Her hair is cropped close.*]

GIRL: O if I were her, and she were me

Jewels on my hair, my finger and my knee
In my ears the dangles, on my wrists the bangles
My sandals will be jewelled, my hair will be dressed;
My perfumes will be milled, my talcums of the best.
On my soups I will be keen
No fish-heads to be seen
O for her to be me
So that I could be free!

[ANOWA *glides out unseen. The* BOY *and the* GIRL *stand looking at each other. The* GIRL'*s eyes glisten with unshed tears while the* BOY *breathes deeply and loudly a couple of times.*]

BOY: Being a woman, of course, that's all you would think about. Though if I were you and so beautiful, I would not worry. Perhaps Father will take you for wife.

GIRL: *Chiaa, aa,* that man who is afraid of women?

BOY: Listen, it is dangerous talking to you. How can you say a fearful thing like that?

GIRL: But I am not lying … they say … they say …

BOY: Shut up. [*He hits her on her buttocks, runs down lower right and away with the* GIRL *pursuing him, her broom raised. From upper left,* ANOWA *re-enters the hall.*]

ANOWA: [*To the now disappeared* GIRL *and* BOY] You said it right, my child. But the elders gave the ruling before you and even I came: 'The string of orphan beads might look better on the wrist of the leopard but it is the antelope who has lost his mother.'

[*She wanders round aimlessly, humming to herself. Presently, Panyin-na-Kakra enter. They are about eight years old. They run in from upper right with ostrich feather fans, stand on either side of the gilded chair and automatically begin fanning the chair. This goes on for some time without* ANOWA *noticing it. When she does, she laughs out dryly.*]

ANOWA: Poor children, I feel like picking them up and carrying them on my back.

PANYIN-NA-KAKRA: [*Still fanning*] Mother please, we did not hear you.

ANOWA: It is all right, my children, I was not speaking to you. [*Aside*] They are fanning that chair now so that by the time their lord enters, the space around it will be cool. I suppose this is one of the nice things Yaako is teaching them to do. Hmm … woe the childless woman, they warn. Let someone go and see their mother, who is she? Where is she sitting while they stand here fanning an empty chair? Let someone go and see how she suffered bearing them. The nine months dizziness, when food tasted like dung and water like urine. Nine months of unwholesome desires and evil dreams. Then the hour of the breaking of the amnion, when the space between her life and her death wore thin like a needy woman's hair thread. O the stench of old blood gone hot … Did she go through all that and with her rest at the end postponed so they [*pointing at the boys*] will come and fan an empty chair? To fan an empty chair? [*She gets up and listlessly goes to the Picture of Queen Victoria and addresses it.*]
Hei, sister, I hear you are a queen. Maybe in spite of the strange look of you, you are a human woman, too, eh? How is it with you over there? Do you sometimes feel like I feel, that you should not have been born? Nana … won't you answer? If you won't answer [*making gesture of riddance*] take your headache … and I say, you don't have to look at me like that because I have seen your likes before. [*To herself*] But I shall not cry. I shall not let him see the tears from my eyes. Someone should have taught me how to grow up to be a woman. I hear in other lands a woman is nothing. And they let her know this from the day of her birth. But here, O my spirit mother, they let a girl grow up as she pleases until she is married. And then she is like any woman anywhere: in order for her man to be a man, she must not think, she must not talk. O—o, why didn't someone teach me how to grow up to be a woman? [*Then she remembers the children.*] *Hei,* Kakra, Panyin! Stop fanning that chair.

PANYIN-NA-KAKRA: [*Startled*] But please, Mother, Yaako said …

ANOWA: I say. Stop fanning that chair Panyin, go and tell

Yaako that I have asked you to stop fanning the chair. [*They put their fans on one of the stools and* PANYIN *goes out.* ANOWA *puts her arms around* KAKRA *and moves down with him. When she sits down he sits on a rug by her.*] Kakra.

KAKRA: Mother.

ANOWA: Where do you and Panyin come from?

KAKRA: The house in Tantri, Mother.

ANOWA: No, I mean before that.

KAKRA: Mother, I don't know.

ANOWA: Kakra, am I growing old?

KAKRA: [*He turns to look at her and then looks away bewildered.*] Mother, I don't know.

ANOWA: No, you don't know. Go and play with your friends, child.

[KAKRA *rises up and leaves.* ANOWA *bows down her head.* KOFI AKO *enters on the arm* of BOY. *He is bedecked as in the last scene.* ANOWA *stares contemptuously at the two* of *them.* BOY *leads him to the chair and places him in it. Now and any other time in the rest* of *the scene, when* KOFI AKO *silently examines his limbs, 'Asem yi se nea mokobo tuo' or any African funeral march or drums should be played.*]

BOY: Father, shall I go and fetch Nana the priest?

KOFI AKO: [*Hurriedly*] Not yet. I shall call you and send you with a message for him.

BOY: Yes, Father. [*He retires.*]

[*Awkward silence.*]

ANOWA: I was told that you wanted to speak to me.

KOFI AKO: All I want to say Anowa, is that I do not like seeing you walking around the house like this.

ANOWA: You don't like seeing me walk around the house like what?

KOFI AKO: Please, stop asking me annoying questions.

ANOWA: Don't shout. After all, it is you who are anxious that the slaves should not hear us. What I don't understand, Kofi, is why you want to have so many things your own way.

KOFI AKO: [*Very angrily*] And I don't think there is a single woman in the land who speaks to her husband the way you to do me. [*Sighs and relaxes*] Why are you like this, Anowa? Why? [ANOWA *laughs*] Can't you be like other normal women? Other normal people? [ANOWA *continues laughing, then stops abruptly.*]

ANOWA: I still don't know what you mean by normal. Is it abnormal to want to continue working?

KOFI AKO: Yes, if there is no need to.

ANOWA: But my husband, is there a time when there is no need for a human being to work? After all, our elders said that one never stops wearing hats on a head which still stands on its shoulders.

KOFI AKO: I do not see the reason why I should go walking through forests, climbing mountains and crossing rivers to buy skins when I have bought slaves to do just that for me.

ANOWA: And so we come back to where we have been for a long time now. My husband, we did not have to put the strength of our bodies into others. We should not have bought the slaves …

KOFI AKO: But we needed them to do the work for us.

[ANOWA *begins to pace up and down and from side to side and never stops for too long any time during the rest of the scene.*]

ANOWA: As though other people are horses! And now look at us. We do nothing from the crowing of the cock to the setting of the sun. I wander around like a ghost and you sit, washed and oiled like a … bride on show or a god being celebrated. Is this what we left Yebi for? Ah, my husband, where did our young lives go?

KOFI AKO: [*Angrily*] Stop it, Anowa, stop it. And what is the meaning of all this strange talk? If you feel old, that is your own affair. I feel perfectly young.

ANOWA: Do you?

KOFI AKO: [*Fiercely*] Yes, I do. And you stop creeping around the house the way you do. Like some beggar. Making yourself a laughing stock. Can't you do anything to yourself? After all, you are my wife.

ANOWA: Am I your wife? What is there to prove it?

KOFI AKO: I don't understand you.

ANOWA: Don't you? I am asking you what I do or what there is about me that shows I am your wife. I do not think putting on fine clothes is enough.

KOFI AKO: Are you referring to the fact that we have not had children?

ANOWA: An adopted child is always an adopted child and a slave child, a slave … Perhaps I am the barren one. But you deserve a son; so Kofi, I shall get you a wife. One of these plump mulatto women of Oguaa …

KOFI AKO: Anowa, Stop that!

ANOWA: Besides, such women are more civilised than I, who only come from Yebi. They, like you, have learned the ways of the white people. And a woman like that may be attractive enough to be allowed into your bed …

KOFI AKO: Anowa stop that! Stop it, stop it!

ANOWA: [*Laughing*] Stop what? Stop what?

[KOFI AKO *sighs again and relaxes. He begins to examine his limbs as the funeral music or drums rise and fall, and* ANOWA *plays at digging her toes into the skins or re-arranging the plates on the sideboard.*]

And what did the priest say the last time he was here?

KOFI AKO: What do you mean? What has that to do with you?

ANOWA: Too much. I know all this has something to do with what he has been telling you.

KOFI AKO: You are speaking as if your head is not there.

ANOWA: [*Screaming*] What did his divination say about me?

KOFI AKO: I don't know. And anyway, listen. I thought you were just as good at this sort of thing as he is. You should know, should you not? Why don't you go and wash your mouth so you can be a priestess at last. I can't stand any more of your strange ways.

ANOWA: [*Voice betraying nervousness*] What are you talking about?

KOFI AKO: [*Laughing bitterly*] What am I talking about!

[*Another awkward pause*]

ANOWA: Yes, what are you talking about?

KOFI.AKO: [*With an almost feigned fatigue*] Please, just leave me alone. O God, Anowa did you have to destroy me too? What does someone like you want from life? Anowa, did you … I mean did you make me just to destroy me?

ANOWA: Kofi, what are you saying?

KOFI AKO: Anowa, Anowa, O, Anowa.

ANOWA: So what did the priest say the last time he was here?

KOFI AKO: That has nothing to do with you.

ANOWA: I think it has. Too much, I feel deep inside me that all this business about me leaving you has something to do with what he told you last week.

KOFI AKO: What mad talk!

ANOWA: [*Hysterically*] What did the priest's divination say about me?

KOFI AKO: Please stop walking up and down. It irritates me.

ANOWA: Why are you sending me away from you?

KOFI AKO: Just leave me alone.

ANOWA: What have I done wrong?

KOFI AKO: Nothing.

ANOWA: Is it because I did not give you children?

[*Silence. She moves up to him and changes her attitude to one of supplication.*]

Do you want to take a new wife who would not like to see me around?

KOFI AKO: Anowa, why do you want to go on asking foolish questions to which you know I cannot give you answers?

ANOWA: But they are not foolish questions.

KOFI AKO: [*Unconcerned*] In fact, I thought you would be glad to get away. I don't know what you want, and even if I knew, I am not sure it would have been in my power to give it. And you can't give me the only thing I want from you, a child. Let us part, Anowa.

ANOWA: But going away is one thing. Being sent away is another.

KOFI AKO: And by that you mean, as always, that you have a right to do what you like and as always I am to sit by and watch?

ANOWA: [*She throws up her hands in despair.*] O the god of our fathers! Is there nothing I can open my mouth to say which cannot be twisted around my own neck to choke me?

[*Music or drums as* KOFI AKO *examines his limbs.* ANOWA *paces up and down. Then she speaks, almost to herself.*]

ANOWA: Did the priest say … what is there about me which he thinks will not bring you blessings now? I must have done something wrong. I must have done something. I'm not a child. Kofi, I know they say a man whose wife is constantly sleeping with other men does not prosper. Did the priest say I am doing something like that? Or anything as evil as that?

KOFI AKO: [*A bitter smile on his lips*] Just go away and leave me alone, woman.

ANOWA: [*Sadly*] I cannot, my husband. Because I have nowhere to go. I swore I would not go back to Yebi. And I can still live here, can I not? I would not disturb you. I can stay in my part of the house. Just don't send me away, we have not seen each other's beds for far too long for it to matter if we don't any more …

[*She stares at him and utters her next words as though she has just made a discovery.*]

ANOWA: A—h—h or is it a death you are dying? We are dying. Listen, my husband, did the priest say you are dying, I am dying, we are dying?

KOFI AKO: You are mad. I am very alive.

ANOWA: [*She gets up and raises her voice*] Boy!

KOFI AKO: Why are you calling him?

ANOWA: It has nothing to do with you.

BOY: [*Running in*] Mother, I am here.

ANOWA: Boy, I am going to ask you a question. [*She resumes pacing up and down.*] Boy, you know your master says I must go away from here and never come back. [BOY *hangs his head down with embarrassment.*] My feet are on the road already and if it were not that he has not yet told me what he has found wrong with me or what I have done wrong, I would already be gone. Boy, do you know why?

BOY: No, Mother.

ANOWA: Boy, have you heard of a man who seeks to divorce his wife and will not say why?

BOY: Mother, I have never known the customs of this land well.

ANOWA: What about where you came from? Did you hear of such a case before you were taken away?

BOY: I do not remember that I did.

ANOWA: Boy, I thank you. Go call for me as many of the older men and women as are around ... Bring everybody on whom your eyes fall.

BOY: Yes, Mother. [*He leaves.*]

KOFI AKO: [*Furiously*] Anowa, what are you doing? Why must they know about this? You have never behaved like a child before – why are you behaving like one now?

ANOWA: I do not know why we must not bring them in. I need their help and they also came from places where men live, eat and die. Perhaps one is among them who can help me. And I am behaving like a child now because I have gained nothing from behaving like a grown-up all my life.

KOFI AKO: [*Surprised*] You are mad Anowa.

ANOWA: Not yet!

BOY: [*From doorway*] Are they to come?

ANOWA: Let them come.

[BOY *re-enters followed by as many men and women as possible. The last pair is the twins. They all shuffle around looking wide-eyed.*]

ALL: Mother, we are here.

ANOWA: I see you. Listen. Has any of you heard of a woman whose husband wanted to divorce her but would not tell her why? [*They look bewildered and answer 'No' as if it were a line in a musical round, sung softly: No, no, no, no, no, no … They all whisper aloud to each other.*] Then please you may go … [*They all turn round at once.*] No wait … Eh—eh … I would like to send some of you. I am sending you to the oldest and wisest people on this land; go ask them if they have ever heard of a man who sought to divorce his wife and would not tell her why. [*Points at random to different people*] You go to the bearded woman of Kwaakrom and you to the old priests of Nanaam Mpow. You over there to Bekoe, he whom dwarfs abducted and taught the mysteries of the woods. Go quickly and come back today and walk as you have never walked before. Come quickly, for already I hear too many noises in my head and you must come back before my mind flies and gets lost. [*The crowd disperses through all available exits. Exhausted but still excited,* ANOWA *paces around* KOFI AKO *who is now very silent.*] I have known this was coming for weeks and I have feared. An old man said, 'Fear "it-is-coming" but not "It-has-come" '. But for me 'it-has-come' has brought me no peace. Perhaps … Boy!

BOY: [*Running*] Mother, I am here.

ANOWA: I hear Nana Abakrampahene Kokroko is here. He and the other chiefs are meeting with the Governor. Go. Whisper in his ears that he is to come to me. Tell him it is urgent and he is to pardon us for not going to him ourselves. All shall be explained in time. He is to come but without his retinue.

KOFI AKO: [*Raising himself up*] Anowa, what are you doing all this for?

ANOWA: The times are past when our individual actions had to be explained to each other.

[BOY *looks away in embarrassment.*]

KOFI AKO: Perhaps you are going out of your senses.

ANOWA: That should not mean anything to you.

KOFI AKO: That is not what concerns me, but you shall not let this out before Nana. [*He stamps his feet.*]

ANOWA: Just sit there and look at me.

KOFI AKO: [*Shouts*] You may go away, Boy. Forget what your Mother told you.

BOY: Yes Father. [*He retires.*]

ANOWA: Who are you to say what you shall allow and what you shall not allow me?

KOFI AKO: [*Loud with anger*] Nana is my friend and not yours.

ANOWA: That is why I am asking him to come.

KOFI AKO: Anowa, you shall not disgrace me before him.

ANOWA: Darkness has overtaken us already, and does it matter if we hit each against the other? Are you not disgracing me before the whole world?

KOFI AKO: Your strange speeches will not persuade me …

ANOWA: I am not trying to. It is a long time since my most ordinary words ceased to have any meaning for me.

KOFI AKO: I say once more that Nana is the only man in this world I respect and honour.

ANOWA: My good husband, in the old days how well I knew you. That is why I want to consult him too.

KOFI AKO: I should have known that you were always that clever.

ANOWA: And certain things have shown that cleverness is not a bad thing.

KOFI AKO: Everyone said you were a witch. I should have believed them.

ANOWA: [*Derisively*] Why, have I choked you with the bone of an infant?

KOFI AKO: Stop all this show and just leave me alone, I say.

ANOWA: Then I shall ask advice of whom I please.

KOFI AKO: Anowa, if you do not leave me quietly, but go consulting anybody about this affair, I shall brand you a witch.

ANOWA: [*Shocked*] No!

KOFI AKO: [*Brought suddenly to life by her exclamation*] And if I do, you know there is more than one person in the world who would believe me.

ANOWA: [*Screams*] No, no, no!

KOFI AKO: And there will be those who would be prepared to furnish proof.

ANOWA: Kofi, I am not hearing you right.

KOFI AKO: And then you know what could happen. But, that should not make much difference to you. Since you do not care to live or behave like everybody else ...

ANOWA: But what have I done?

KOFI AKO: I just want you to leave me, that's all.

ANOWA: O the Gods of my fathers, what is it? What is it?

KOFI AKO: I shall have the little house built for you, as I promised, but in Yebi ...

ANOWA: But I cannot go and live there.

KOFI AKO: I will give you half of the trade and half of the slaves, if you want them.

ANOWA: I don't want anything from you.

KOFI AKO: Take away with you all the jewelry.

ANOWA: I say I want nothing ...

KOFI AKO: And you must leave immediately. I myself shall come to Yebi, or send people you can respect to come and explain everything to your family ...

ANOWA: No, no, no!

KOFI AKO: ... I shall ask a few men and women to go with you now, and carry your personal belongings.

ANOWA: But ...

KOFI AKO: Boy!

ANOWA: Stop!

KOFI AKO: What? [*Unknown to the two, not only* BOY *but several of the slaves, men and women, appear.*]

ANOWA: You cannot send me away like this. Not to Yebi, or anywhere. Not before you have told me why. I swore to Mother I was not returning. Not ever. [*Not shedding a tear but her eyes shining dangerously*] No, I am not in rags. But ... but I do not have children from this marriage. Ah! Yes, Kofi, [*she moves to him and whispers hoarsely and audibly*] we do not have children, Kofi, we have not got children! And for years now, I have not seen your bed. And Kofi, [*getting hysterical*] now that I think back on it, you have never been interested in any other woman ...

KOFI AKO: What are you saying, Anowa?

ANOWA: Kofi, are you dead? [*Pause*] Kofi, is your manhood

gone? I mean, you are like a woman. [*Pause*] Kofi, there is not hope any more, is there? [*Pause*] Kofi … tell me, is that why I must leave you? That you have exhausted your masculinity acquiring slaves and wealth?

[*Silence*]

Why didn't you want me to know? You could have told me. Because we were friends. Like brother and sister. You just did not want me to know? And the priest said it was my fault. That I ate your manhood up? Why did he say I did it? Out of envy? Did he not tell you that perhaps you had consumed it up yourself acquiring wealth and slaves?

[KOFI *looks around and sees the peeping eyes. He is horrified. He gestures to* ANOWA *who doesn't know what is happening and goes on talking. He makes an attempt to go away and then sits down again. The slaves disappear.*]

ANOWA: Now I know. So that is it. My husband is a woman now. [*She giggles.*] He is a corpse. He is dead wood. But less than dead wood because at least, that sometimes grows mushrooms … Why didn't you want me to know? [*Long pause while they look at each other strangely. Then he gets up to leave.*] Where are you going? Kofi, don't leave. [*Pause*] Let us start from the beginning. [*Long pause*] No, I shall leave you in peace. [*Pause*] I am leaving, Kofi. I am leaving. I shall leave you in peace.

[*He exits upper left. She watches his receding back until he disappears. She then shifts her gaze to the gilded chair. She stares at that for some time, after which her eyes just wander in general around the room. Then at some point she begins to address the furniture.*]

ANOWA: Ah, very soon the messengers will be coming back,
Rugs, pictures, you, chair and you, Queen,
Should they ask of me from you, tell them I am gone,
Tell them it matters not what the wise ones say,
For
Now, I am wiser than they.

[*She fixes her eyes on the gilded chair again. Suddenly she jumps a step or two and sits in it and begins to dangle her legs like a child, with a delighted grin on her face. She breaks into a giggle. There is a sudden gun-shot offstage, followed by a stillness. As pandemonium breaks out offstage with women and men shrieking,* ANOWA *begins to giggle again. The light dies slowly on her.*

Lights come on both parts of the stage. Upper is still the great hall. In the centre is the gilded chair unoccupied. In the background can be heard funeral drums and wailing. A few women, led by BADUA, *who is weeping, troop in from upper right and sit down,* BADUA *in the right-hand corner nearest the lower stage. The women sit around the gilded chair as though it is the funeral bed. A little later,* OSAM *enters from upper left to sit in the left hand corner facing* BADUA. *All are in deep red mourning. The drums and wailing stop, but only to give way to Kofi's* HORNBLOWER *who enters immediately after* OSAM, *stands directly behind the chair, blows a sequence of the exhortation and stops. The lights go dim on the upper stage.*

THE-MOUTH-THAT-EATS-SALT-AND-PEPPER *enters.* OLD WOMAN *first and almost shrieking.*]

OLD WOMAN: *Puei, puei, puei!* This is the type of happening out of which we get stories and legends. Yebi, I wish you *dué, dué, dué.* May all the powers that be condole with you. Kofi Ako shoots himself and Anowa drowns herself! This is too much. Other villages produce great men, men of wealth, men of name. Why should this befall us? What tabooed food have we eaten? What unholy ground have we trodden?

[OLD MAN *enters, stands in the centre of the stage with his head down.*]

O Kofi Ako! Some say he lost his manhood because he was not born with much to begin with; that he had been a sickly infant and there always was only a hollow in him where a man's strength should be. Others say he had consumed it acquiring wealth, or exchanged it for prosperity. But I say that all should be laid at Anowa's doorstep. What man prospers, married to a woman like Anowa? Eh, would even Amanfi the giant have retained his strength faced with that witch? They say she always worked as though she could eat a thousand cows. Let the gods forgive me for speaking ill of the dead, but Anowa ate Kofi Ako up!

OLD MAN: [*Looking at her keenly, he chuckles.*] There is surely one thing we know how to do very well. And that is assigning blame when things go wrong.

OLD WOMAN: What do you mean by that! I did not shoot Kofi Ako, did I?

OLD MAN: I never said you did.

OLD WOMAN: Was it not that Anowa who made him shoot himself?

OLD MAN: [*Quietly and not looking at* OLD WOMAN] Perhaps, perhaps, perhaps. And yet no one goes mad in emptiness, unless he has the disease already in his head from the womb. No. It is men who make men mad. Who knows if Anowa would have been a better woman, a better person if we had not been what we are?

[OLD WOMAN *glares at him, spits and wobbles out coughing harder than ever before.*]

They used to say here that Anowa behaved as though she were a heroine in a story. Some of us wish she had been happier and that her life had not had so much of the familiar human scent in it. She is true to herself. She refused to come back here to Yebi, to our gossiping and our judgements. Osam and Badua have gone with the others to bring the two bodies home to Yebi. Ow, if there is life after death, Anowa's spirit will certainly have something to say about that!

[*He begins to walk away, while all the lights begin to die.*]

In the approaching darkness, we hear the single Atentenben wailing in loneliness.

Notes

Summary

The action in Phase Three takes place in Kofi Ako's big house at Oguaa. Kofi Ako is now very rich. He has many slaves and has taken on the status of a chief. He is called 'Nana' and 'master of the earth'. He is carried in a procession across the stage, wearing a crown, jewellery and expensive clothes.

Anowa enters, still wearing her old clothes and bare-footed as always. She tells how, when she was about twelve years old, her grandmother spoke to her about the white men, the building of castles and forts along the coast, and the trade in human beings. She came to understand that good people try to forget that evil trade. She also tells of the dream she had about how the white men came to Africa and made slaves of African men and women. Since then, even the mention of a slave affects her emotionally.

The next scene takes place between two slaves, a boy and a girl. They speak of how people gossip that Anowa is a witch. From the Boy and the Girl we learn that Kofi Ako has refused to talk to his wife; he has also refused to let her share his bed, and, without giving any reason, he has asked her to go away.

While they are talking about her, Anowa enters quietly, overhears some of their conversation, then leaves, returning as they go out.

Next, Panyin-Na-Kakra, the eight-year-old twin brothers, enter. They begin to fan Kofi Ako's empty chair, to cool the air around it. When Anowa notices this, she feels sorry for them, and tells them to stop fanning the chair.

Kofi Ako enters, still dressed in his fine clothes. He feels that his wife must obey every instruction he gives, and that Anowa should respect his superiority as the man in the house. Anowa hates the fact that she no longer has work to do, now that everything is done by the slaves. The situation develops into a crisis. Kofi Ako is angry because Anowa does not behave as he feels a wife should behave.

Anowa feels differently. To her, there is nothing to show that she is a wife. Their marriage is without a child. Whether or not she is the barren one, she challenges Kofi Ako to have children with other women.

Anowa wonders whether it is because of something the priest's divination has told Kofi Ako about her, that he has decided to send her away to Yebi. Their love has turned sour. Now they see each other as enemies. Kofi Ako simply wants Anowa to leave him alone. Anowa now feels angry and disappointed. She sends for as many as possible of the older people from around the place, so that she can ask them whether any of them has 'heard of a woman whose husband wanted to divorce her but would not tell her why' (p.83). She becomes more and more distressed and wants to send for other wise people, including Nana Abakrampahene Kokroko, a chief who is a friend of Kofi Ako. The argument becomes stronger, and Kofi Ako threatens to brand Anowa a witch (p.85) unless she goes back to Yebi.

Anowa, becoming more and more hysterical, protests that she cannot return to Yebi. She swore never to go back; she has no children; she has not seen Kofi Ako's bed for years. As she speaks, she remembers that Kofi Ako has never been interested in other women, and she realises that he has exhausted his masculinity acquiring slaves and wealth. He is 'dead'; his manhood is gone; he is a 'corpse' and 'less than dead wood because at least that sometimes grows mushrooms' (pp.86–87).

As she speaks, others have been coming back into the room, and have heard what she said. Kofi Ako cannot stand the disgrace and shame. He goes out of the room. Anowa remains, in a strange state of mind. She begins to talk to the furniture, saying:

> Should they ask of me from you, tell them I am gone,
> Tell them it matters not what the wise ones say,
> For
> Now, I am wiser than they. (p.87)

She goes and sits in Kofi Ako's throne and we hear the sound as Kofi Ako, outside, shoots himself dead. The lights go off.

Badua and Osam and a funeral procession come in. Anowa is not there. The-Mouth-That-Eats-Salt-And-Pepper enters, and the Old Woman tells us that Anowa has drowned herself and that Osam and Badua have come to bring the bodies back to Yebi for burial. The Old Woman feels that everything is Anowa's fault, and that she 'ate Kofi Ako up'. The Old Man is gentler, saying:

> It is men who make men mad. Who knows if Anowa would have been a better woman, a better person if we had not been what we are? (p.89)

Review Questions

When you are answering these questions, always try to find words from the play to support your answers.

1 List the items that decorate the central hall in the Big House at Oguaa. What is the importance of each of them?

2 What do the Hornblower and the women who accompany him add to Kofi Ako's position?

3 In a long **soliloquy** Anowa recalls her past experience as a young child with her grandmother (pp.69–72). Read the passage, then answer the following questions:

- a What is a soliloquy?
- b What questions does Anowa ask her grandmother?
- c How would you describe the grandmother's treatment of Anowa?
- d Anowa could be described here as 'inquisitive'. What is meant by that?
- e Anowa had a dream. What did she see and feel in her dream?
- f What was the effect of this dream on Anowa and the household?
- g Do you agree that Anowa should have been a priestess? What are your reasons?
- h Describe Anowa's present state of mind.

4 What is the Boy's attitude to what the Girl says about Anowa and Kofi Ako?

5 Panyin-Na-Kakra fan an empty chair. (p.76)

- a Why do they do that?
- b What does that tell you about Kofi Ako?
- c How does Anowa react to what they are doing?
- d Anowa describes in detail the condition of a woman who carries a baby in her womb (p.77). What are some of the points you remember?
- e Of what is the empty chair, fanned by the children, a **symbol**? (See *Symbolism* p.20.)

6 What does Anowa's action in public (pp.86–87) do to the image of Kofi Ako? What does Anowa suddenly realise about Kofi Ako, which makes him go away and shoot himself?

Exercises

1 In appearance, and in the way they carry themselves at the beginning of Phase Three, Kofi Ako and Anowa are in sharp **contrast**. Explain.
2 What does the conversation between the Boy and the Girl reveal about the relationship between Anowa and Kofi Ako?
3 In what ways does the Girl resemble Anowa as she was a long time ago?
4 What do you think are the main reasons why Anowa drowns herself?

Activity

The beginning of Phase Three reminds us of the celebration of a traditional festival. Ask your parents or guardians the name of the traditional festival celebrated in your community. How did it all begin? Why do people celebrate it? At what time of year does it take place? Find out as many other details as you can. Find out how it is celebrated from beginning to end. Describe the final big occasion – the grand durbar of Chiefs – to your class.

General Questions

When you are answering these questions, always try to find words from the play to support your answers.

1 Which of the following is **not** true about where the play is set?
   a It is a coastal settlement
   b The people are both farmers and fishermen
   c There is only one beautiful mountain
   d The action of the play is in the 1990s
2 Kofi Ako is described as lazy because
   a he has built a house at Oguaa
   b he trades in skins
   c he wants other people to work for him
   d he is handsome and wealthy
3 From the play we learn that
   a Anowa should have been a priestess
   b Kofi Ako married a mulatto woman
   c the Old Woman likes Anowa
   d Anowa is very lazy
4 Anowa does not want Kofi Ako to make slaves of other human beings because

- a she fears they will take her husband from her
- b slaves don't work hard
- c it is evil
- d she is a witch

5 Kofi Ako is described as tall and broad, but Anowa is small in size. This difference between the two makes
- a tension
- b conflict
- c climax
- d contrast

Use the following conversation to answer Questions 6 to 9.

Speaker A: Mother, I do not know what is wrong with you.
Speaker B: And how would you know what is wrong with me? Look here, … marriage is like a piece of cloth …
Speaker A: I like mine and it is none of your business. (p.37)

6 Who is Speaker A?
- a Kofi Ako
- b Osam
- c Badua
- d Anowa

7 Who is Speaker B?
- a Badua
- b Osam
- c Anowa
- d Kofi Ako

8 This conversation is
- a an agreement
- b a conflict
- c a monologue
- d a setting

9 What relation is Speaker B to Speaker A?
- a Wife
- b Daughter
- c Mother
- d Father

10 Which one of the following do we learn from the drama?
- a Money is not the only thing that can bring happiness to a family
- b Women slaves are stronger that men slaves
- c It is more painful to die by drowning than by shooting oneself
- d Impotence brings happiness to families

11 Which of the following does **not** show that the play is set in Ghana?
- a The names of the characters
- b The town of Oguaa
- c The use of Odomankoma
- d The Prologue

12 The play is introduced by the Old Man. His speech is part of the
- a proverb
- b story
- c prologue
- d monologue

13 The character who is described as ‘Beautiful as Korado Ahima’ is
- a Badua
- b Kofi Ako
- c Osam
- d Anowa

14 What sort of a woman do the people in the village see Anowa as?
- a Happy
- b Strange
- c Friendly
- d Sad

15 Anowa and Kofi Ako are unable to have children because
- a there is a curse on Anowa
- b Kofi Ako is a slave master
- c Kofi Ako is impotent
- d Anowa is a priestess

16 The play is a tragedy because
- a Badua makes Osam very unhappy
- b Kofi Ako is a descendant of white men
- c Kofi Ako and Anowa run away
- d The main character dies

17 The twins fan Kofi Ako’s empty chair in order to cool the air around it. What is this action a **symbol** of?
- a Kofi Ako has lost his manhood

b Kofi Ako is the new chief of Yebi
c It is too hot in Oguaa
d Slaves must always work

18 The main character in the play is
a Osam
b Badua
c Anowa
d the Old Man

19 Which of the following is true about Kofi Ako?
a He likes to work hard
b He has no respect for women's views
c He has too many wives
d He married Anowa in the traditional way

20 Why does Kofi Ako shoot himself?
a He feels ashamed of himself
b Anowa refuses to go away
c One of his slaves died
d Anowa divorced him

Exercise

Three **themes** were discussed in the Introductory section (pp.14–17):

1 The result or consequences of disobeying one's parents out of pride.
2 Happiness in a family cannot be bought with riches and wealth – love and care are more important.
3 Human beings, especially children and those we call slaves, must be treated with dignity.

What other themes can you find in the play?